apartment therapy

apartment

therapy

The

Eight

Step

Home

Cure

Maxwell Gillingham-Ryan

Bantam Books

APARTMENT THERAPY
A Bantam Book / April 2006

Published by
Bantam Dell
A Division of Random House, Inc.
New York, New York

Book design by Patrice Sheridan
Illustrations by Emily Payne

Library of Congress Cataloging-in-Publication Data
Gillingham-Ryan, Maxwell.
Apartment therapy : the eight step home cure /
Maxwell Gillingham-Ryan.
p. cm.
Includes bibliographical references and text.
ISBN-13: 978-0-553-38312-6
ISBN-10: 0-553-38312-4
1. Interior decoration—Psychological aspects. I. Title.
NK2113 .G56 2006
747.01'9—dc22   2005053597

Printed in the United States of America
Published simultaneously in Canada

www.bantamdell.com

BVG   10 9 8 7 6 5 4 3 2 1

Contents

Acknowledgments

All my thanks and gratitude to:

Sara Kate, my wife, who helped me declutter my writing countless times and continues to inspire me with new ways of creating a healthy home.

My mother and father, who gave me my first home, filled with art and dinner parties, and to my stepmother, who taught my father and the rest of us how to keep it clean.

My brother, for sharing rooms since we were little and for seeing that Apartment Therapy would be a great blog.

Emily Payne, for bringing the words to life with simple, beautiful illustrations.

Jasie, for your careful, thoughtful reading of a very long manuscript and all your great ideas for shortening it.

Eric and Thea, for offering your home for our winter writers' retreat, and allowing me to take up the entire dining room.

Philip Rappaport, the most enthusiastic editor an amateur writer could ever wish to have, for giving the book a home.

Wendy Silbert, my most diligent agent, who believed in this book from the very beginning, taught me how to write a book proposal, and ensured that it became a reality.

All of my clients and students, for allowing me to visit the most personal of spaces, your home. It is because of you and for you that this book is written.

Introduction

In the café next door to my apartment where I often have breakfast, I met Myles, a film editor who lives a few blocks away. When I told him that I was an interior designer and an "apartment therapist" who worked with regular people in regular apartments, our casual conversation quickly changed. He wanted to tell me about his apartment and see what I thought.

"Would you mind?" he asked.

"Not at all," I said. "What's the problem?"

Within minutes, with very little prompting, I was deep into a story about Myles's breakup with his girlfriend and how she had recently moved out, leaving him with a very nice apartment that he hated. The memories were so painful that he couldn't sleep in his bedroom and was considering moving.

Myles had an intuitive understanding that his personal troubles were somehow linked to the space he lived in. He knew that he had to change his home in order to feel better. He wanted help.

We talked more, and I asked him if he had done anything at all with his apartment to make it better. He had. He had moved his bed out into the living room and added some color to the walls. The apartment had been a "drab white box" before, he said. I congratulated him on the color and suggested he take this further, but told him that he should move his bed back into the bedroom. He balked at this idea.

Myles was feeling blocked by his recent breakup and wanted to regain confidence and movement in his own life. Adding color would do this, but settling into a defensive position in the living room would not. I told him that he needed to reclaim his bedroom. I also told him there were three basic things that he could do to move back into the bedroom: perform a deep cleaning, remove any of her personal effects or decorations, and add new color and more light to the room. If that didn't work, I would be happy to visit and see what more could be done.

It worked.

Over the next few weeks we met now and then for coffee, and I would consult as Myles filled me in on the progress he was making at home. His enthusiasm for the project was noticeable and in stark contrast to the depression I had noticed when I first encountered him. Physically moving furniture was creating movement in his life. In the end, Myles transformed his bedroom and reestablished himself in a home that was now his, not "his and hers." Ironically, but not surprisingly, a few months later he received a big editing job in Los Angeles and had to sublet his apartment for the summer. When you get your house in order, other parts of your life just start to follow.

There is a great deal of pain surrounding our relationship with our home. In the past five years, I have met many people like Myles who have shared their private struggles with me in order to find a solution. Especially in the city, where apartment living is the norm and people pay so much for so little, they often come to identify their apartments as "second skins," the center of lives they either love or hate.

Despite the fact that our homes are our only refuge, the only place that we can call our own, most of us are unhappy with the places we live in. Even more do not recognize the strong effect they have on our daily lives. Not sleeping well, not cooking at home, being ashamed to have people over, and being stressed out by repairs are all complaints I hear often. When these issues grow or linger, they come to affect our personal lives and careers. Ducking the problems and moving to another apartment is an extreme and often typical solution, but the first things that follow us when we move are our own bad habits and, as they say, our baggage.

This book is about how a home works and what makes it healthy. It goes far beyond surface-oriented decorating instructions and makeover ideas. It is an eight-week program that guides you through the process of turning your home into a beautiful, well-organized, and inspiring environment.

The program enables you to form and maintain good home habits. By the end of your apartment cure you will want to invite others in to share the pleasure of your home.

Interior Design

This book is the fruit of my experience in two unlikely fields. While rearranging rooms and designing space has always been a passion, my first job was for an interior design company, but it almost ruined my love for design forever.

A week after my college graduation, I went to work for a reputable interior design firm in New York City. Every day I was part of a team that designed wallpaper, sheets, lamps, rugs, and chairs. At first, I found working in a place surrounded by talented and experienced designers inspiring, but soon I began to feel that the projects I was working on were missing something. Although we paid great attention to the patterns and colors of our designs as we busily sketched them out on paper, we thought very little about what happened once our designs were manufactured, sold, and actually used. The "market" for all these products was faceless, and our production seemed to me more of a game than an answer to a problem. There was an emptiness to what I was doing.

That August, I was invited to my boss's house in the Hamptons for a dinner party. His house was beautiful and glowing with candles, some floating in the pool beside our dinner table. It was obvious that a lot of work and money had gone into the evening, from the numerous changes of dinnerware to the orchids that dotted the room. But while the space was impressive, the gathering lacked warmth and interaction. I felt awkward, and I met other people who felt the same way I did. My boss was remarkable at making things look good, but he was not aware of what it took to make guests feel good, and that environment wasn't helping. Impressive does not always equal comfortable.

Leaving the party that night, I realized that I did not want to follow in my boss's footsteps, as successful in his career as he was. I wanted a more holistic career, one that was concerned with more than what was on the surface. As much as I loved beautiful things, it didn't make sense if they didn't serve to directly enhance the lives they were part of. At that point it seemed to me that there was no room in the decorating business both to be a designer and also to deeply improve people's lives.

Teaching

Five years later I was an elementary school teacher with two master's degrees: one in early American literature from Columbia University and one in education from Antioch University. Being a teacher was a great experience and deeply satisfying. People who knew me often asked if I missed art and design, assuming that teaching was such a departure from my previous career. Actually, it wasn't.

I taught at a Waldorf school and worked every day with its arts-based curriculum. Not only do the traditional subjects such as English, math, and geography incorporate an artistic approach, but teachers pay attention to the design and arrangement of each classroom, including the color of the walls, the shape of the desks, and the storage and care of the pencils. Everything is designed to support the students' learning.

One example of this is that there is very little decoration on the walls and in the halls of a Waldorf school. Random visual stimulation is not considered helpful for concentrating on schoolwork. It was in the Waldorf school that I first began to put my love of interior design together with something deeper: the understanding that not only can an environment be beautiful on the outside, it can also be beautiful on the inside by supporting what we are doing.

A good deal of this understanding comes from the realization that you are much more sensitive to space than you think you are. When you enter a room, you take in everything in front of you like a dry sponge absorbing water. Your body may only travel a certain distance, but your eyes move throughout the room, taking in all parts, including the ceiling, the corners, and the floor under your feet. What you touch and feel as well as what you see enter into you and affect you. As a result, a room can make you feel uncomfortable and distracted, or it can make you feel comfortable and welcome. A room can inspire or confuse. It can make you feel small or big. Rooms are powerful.

This idea is nothing new and was certainly used by our ancestors. Throughout history a consciousness of the power that space has for us has been incorporated into architecture and interior design. For example, the great colleges of England are made of rooms set around gardens, an idea that was borrowed from the Greeks. It was known that while rooms were good for instruction, the garden was best for the philosophical discussion of higher matters. By comparison, writers throughout history have been drawn to small, tight spaces, which support their need for solitude and focus. In another example, some American Indians built underground rooms *(kivas)* that were used exclusively for tribal meetings of the highest importance. In our courtrooms, the formality, direction of seating, and raised position of the judge is different from the democratically raised stage in a political forum: one is meant for solving disputes and the other for deciding on leadership. This is all to say that there is a reason why architects spend so many years studying. Creating a working space is both a science and an art. All of this came together when I worked with children.

Part of my job as a Waldorf teacher was to visit my students at home each year. It allowed me to get to know the families better and to see my students' work environment at home. This was the true beginning of Apartment Therapy.

In visiting students' homes, I came to recognize two common problems. The biggest one was overstimulation. Frequently, this came in the form of too much clutter or too much television and other media; sometimes, but not often, the parents themselves were the cause of an overstimulating environment. The other common problem was a lack of a wholesome rhythm. Many children did not have a nightly family dinner, a regular bedtime, or a full breakfast before school. I never would have expected that these simple things would have such an effect on students' performance in school, but they did. Those children who did better in school were the ones whose families encouraged healthy rhythms and rituals at home.

While these healthy homes did not look alike on the surface, they all shared common traits: they were quiet and organized, and though not necessarily large in terms of square footage, they felt spacious and open. Books and toys were not stuffed into every corner. Framed photographs did not cover every wall. The children's play areas were clearly separated from their study areas.

On one visit, one of my best students, Henry, showed

me his "basketball court," which consisted of a hoop over his bedroom door. The "court" was the result of his keeping his room scrupulously clear of clutter, which he had first done as a chore and now did with enthusiasm because it supported one of his favorite activities. Henry also had a chalkboard in his room, on which he kept careful score of his games. In turn, working with numbers on the chalkboard inspired him to mimic his teacher, and he was soon working out difficult math problems at home and then discussing them with his father over dinner each night.

Another student, Anthony, had wonderful creative energy. He sometimes got highly distracted, but this rarely happened at home because his mother had taken great care to give Anthony a good desk in his room, all the materials he needed for his homework, and a regular work time. There was no television in the house, and everything that hung on the walls had been drawn or made by Anthony, his brother or mother, or a friend of the family.

These homes were very different from my old boss's summer house in the Hamptons, with the beautiful interior and the candles floating in the pool. Neither of these students' homes was really that stylish, and neither was all that attractive in the conventional sense of the word. They both were very modest, and yet they felt good to be in. They were beautiful on the inside. These were homes with rooms that you wanted to stay in.

Years after leaving my job at an interior design company, it was clear to me that beauty had much more to do with how a room supported its occupants than with how it defined a look. Bringing the two halves together was the key.

A New Career

In the summer of 2001, I was at a dinner and fell into a conversation with Alan, a twenty-five-year-old banker, who had recently been given a large apartment as a benefit of his new job. Despite his good fortune, he was deeply distressed.

He told me that he had no furniture yet, and he wanted to create a space that would be both comfortable for friends and nice enough to invite a woman over for dinner. All of a sudden he was concerned with a new concept, how to make his own home. This new apartment didn't feel like one yet.

I knew exactly how he felt. He didn't simply want a bachelor pad; he wanted the beginnings of a home. And although he was successful in the field of finance, he was really challenged when it came to creating a home. Alan reminded me of one of my students having difficulty with a math problem, and I found myself saying, "That's easy. I can help you do that."

Alan, like most people, was looking not solely for nice furniture, but also to put together an apartment that would support his activities and express the new, more mature person he was becoming. Rather than buy furniture for him, I knew I had to get to know Alan better in order to help him discover his personal style.

Working with photographs I took of furniture from stores around the city, I showed Alan a great number of possibilities and watched as his visual vocabulary grew. Gradually, we put together a very attractive living room, dining room, and hallway that fit into Alan's budget and excited him in the process. Through all of this, he began to think about how these different rooms would work, and he started to take seriously the notion that this was his home and not just a crash pad.

In the end, the space that I created with Alan was nothing like mine and did not reflect my own tastes. It was his. It had sprung from what I had learned about Alan and how I had supported his goals. Not only did it look good, it worked well. Soon after we completed the project, Alan was having friends over for social gatherings, and his social life took off. His home was finally working for him.

After meeting as strangers at a dinner table just over a month earlier, I was satisfied that I had helped Alan with much more than a decorating job. I had guided him—just like the students at school—in creating a concept of "home."

Discovering Apartment Therapy

Soon after I worked with Alan, two more people approached me to help them in the same way. It dawned on me that working with people on their apartments was an ideal way of combining my design background with my experience in education. And so that fall, after I'd spent seven years as a teacher, my first business was born.

My new business didn't involve teaching, and it didn't involve traditional decorating or interior design. I didn't even know what to call my company. A friend humorously suggested Apartment Therapy, and the name stuck. It seemed therapeutic because what I was doing was helping people solve their apartment problems for themselves, not doing it for them. The phone has been ringing ever since with calls from people responding to this concept after realizing that what they need is not a decorator but someone who understands what they want their home to be like and who can guide them along the way.

I have also received many calls and e-mails from people far away from New York who want to know if I travel or, barring that, if I know of anyone in their city who does what I do. I wish I did. I have always been at a loss for how to help these people, because although I have met plenty of decorators and organizers, I have never met anyone who does anything similar to Apartment Therapy. That's why I wrote this book. It is a distillation of everything I have learned. It is designed to coach and guide you as you reclaim your home and make it the beautiful, healthy place you want it to be.

What This Book Is About

This book has two parts:

1.   Part One opens up your awareness to the reasons you may be experiencing dissatisfaction and stress in your living spaces right now. These two chapters lay the groundwork for understanding the Eight-Week Cure. They explain the basic premise of the whole-body approach, including the concept of flow.

2.   Part Two is the eight-week Cure itself, which leads you step by step through the process of healing your own home. Since the habits you develop during the eight weeks will become a part of your year-round rhythm, the book's final pages provide you with a calendar for ongoing maintenance.

Note: *Do not start the Cure until you believe you are ready to commit an eight-week block of time to renewing your home. If you are not committed, you can easily lose steam and direction, which can make you feel worse than when you started. Be aware that when you disrupt the balance of your home, surprising emotions and unforeseen problems will arise—but these will be solvable and not derail you as long as you are committed to the end.*

It is a big job to heal your home, but by carefully reading this book, not only will your project be done before you know it, it will change your life.

A Word About New York City and ApartmentTherapy.com

Apartment Therapy began in 2001, literally days before I stood on a street corner and watched the World Trade Center fall. So many people did so much for one another in the weeks following the disaster that we were all amazed at the strength of our community and the power and intelligence such a group effort could unleash. With this in mind, I envisioned Apartment Therapy not just as a service but as a way of continuing to link people together, taking advantage of the tremendous goodwill and expertise that are often overlooked in the busy city.

In 2004 my brother and I launched ApartmentTherapy. com in New York to create a community-based extension of the work I was doing with clients. Specifically a blog and not a typical commercial Web site, ApartmentTherapy. com was created as a free interactive site to allow people to find the resources they need, improve their homes, and share inspiration and decorating ideas with others. Hosted daily by myself, and a small editorial team, it becomes richer each week through input from the growing reader base we serve.

With the success of the blog, I found that readers from

across the country were tuning in. People in houses, bunga-lows, and apartments all turned out to have similar issues, similar questions, and the same enthusiasm for fixing up their homes. Since then, I have started blogs in other cities with the same goal: to make it easier for people to create beautiful, healthy homes through connections to people and resources around them.

Traveling Light

In 1991, I was traveling by bicycle in Italy. On my bicycle I carried everything I thought I needed to live: tent, sleeping bag, insulated mat, stove, cooking pots, repair kit, clothing—you name it, I had it. My bicycle was extremely heavy, but I was traveling for a year, and I wanted to be prepared.

One day during the first month of the trip, another rider rode up and slowed down to greet me. He was a Swiss doctor on a two-week trip to Sicily. He had left Switzerland earlier and was more than halfway through his trip. He was moving swiftly, easily clocking about twice as many miles a day as I was, yet I saw none of the panniers and packs on his bike that I had on mine. In fact, he was barely carrying anything at all. All I saw was a spare tire, an extra inner tube, and a small wallet strapped to his rear rack. It was as if he was out for a day ride, but he was nearly seven hundred miles from home.

Shocked by how light he was traveling and sensing he had more experience, I asked him how he managed. He told me it was easy. Over time he had found that he didn't need anything aside from the little that I saw. He bought his food daily, washed his one set of clothes every night, and hung them up to dry in his room. But what if something happened? I asked. What if he had something besides a minor breakdown or needed warmer clothes? How would he be prepared?

His explanation was inspiring and simple. Rather than relying only on himself, he put his trust in others. Even though he didn't need much, he looked forward to meeting people and asking for help when needed. By carrying so little, he not only moved more easily, he met more people and his experience was far richer. He was truly taking in all of Italy.

Struggling to keep up with him on my heavily laden bike, I saw his point. We weren't traveling through the Arctic Circle; this was Europe. Instead of being prepared, I had overpacked. In all the days I had traveled so far, I hadn't met anyone and had been embarrassed to ask for help. He was traveling <u>in</u> Italy; I was traveling <u>through</u> it.

That afternoon, after sharing a long lunch with wine and cheese, he excused himself to ride on ahead. We said good-bye, and as he slipped away up the road, disappearing out of sight, I felt like a bump on a log. I wished I could have sped up and ridden with him a bit longer, but it was impossible.

The next day I went to the post office and sent home everything I could. Though I will admit to being very nervous about it even as I stripped things from my panniers, I filled two big boxes, and the loss of weight transformed my trip immediately.

It was at that point that I realized that "being prepared" can sometimes be a euphemism for being scared to let go. How much we carry—whether it is on our bicycle, in our bag, or in our home—is often directly related to how little we trust in life to guide us well, and in others to help us out in a pinch. To this day, I have found that traveling light yields a far richer experience.

part **one**

The Home Is a Living Place

Chapter One

Is Your
Home Healthy?

In the first few years that I took on clients, I was surprised by the number of people who were miserable in their homes. I wondered what was going on to cause so much distress. As I visited more houses and apartments and began to read books on shelter style and home improvement, I soon realized that most

American home dwellers tuning in to home improvement are not simply lacking in style or needing to declutter; they are dealing with sick homes.

Despite good intentions, Americans have not only lost touch with how to create and maintain a healthy home, they have created new diseases such as clutter, disposophobia (the fear of letting go of things), and what I call movie theater syndrome and bowling alley syndrome. Like another national health issue, obesity, most of our household issues stem from the fact that we consume too much and work off too little.

As you read this book, I want you to broaden the concept of home and apply to it the same principles we apply to our own bodies. Like the body, the home should be thought of as a living organism. For starters, healthy homes are homes that consume carefully and get regular exercise. After health is established, style and decoration come much more easily and can be seen as natural finishing touches. In fact, style and decoration are extensions of a healthy home. You can't have one without the other.

Hypernesting

Today, Americans spend more money on home improvement than ever before. A whopping twenty-five million Americans took on a home improvement project in 2005, spending $150 billion (2 percent of our GNP). Judging from television shows such as *Trading Spaces, Design on a Dime,* and *This Old House,* Americans can't seem to get enough. And the demand crosses gender lines: shows such as the tremendously popular *Queer Eye for the Straight Guy* attract male and female viewers alike, while

Debbie Travis's *Facelift* on both Oxygen and HGTV attracts a growing number of female homeowners wanting to DIY (do it yourself).

Each year brings new magazines as well. The old-school *Architectural Digest* has been pushed aside by flashier offerings such as *Metropolitan Home* and *Elle Décor,* and they are now being challenged by newcomers with a focus on shopping and affordability, such as *Domino, Budget Living,* and *Bargain Style.* All in all, more Americans than ever are fixing up their homes—and doing the work themselves. In all of this they are trying to retrieve the feeling of home they have lost. But despite the amount of activity and money spent, most of these efforts end in dissatisfaction, because they only treat the symptoms—they don't provide a cure.

In place of creating a healthy home, we are trying to buy solutions and cram too much into our homes. What was modestly termed "cocooning" in the 1970s by trendspotters who saw us spending more recreational time at home has become Hypernesting. Instead of asking ourselves what would really make our home work better, we usually jump to the conclusion that there must be something we can buy to solve our home's challenges—a flatter television screen, a closet organizing system, or color-coded photo albums.

But when we take something new into our home, we rarely let go of something else. This is how our home gains weight, grows unhealthy, and begins to nag at us. Not only have we created some new diseases, we've even created new doctors to treat our problem. Professional organizers and home disaster specialists have sprung up only recently, and their job is to help us sort and manage our extra weight.

Most of us aren't in need of more organizing; we need

to manage our consumption, let go of our stuff, and learn how to restore life to our homes.

I often ask my clients what they imagine their apartment would say to them if it could speak. Samantha, a stockbroker, told me that her home would say, "Can't she see that I am dying? Why doesn't she do anything to save me?" As she said this, we were sitting in a badly lit, cluttered, unfinished room. Embarrassed, Samantha said that she didn't know where to begin. It was one of the best things I had ever heard a client say. Besides being completely honest, I told her, in using the word *begin* she'd hit upon the main issue. The solution was not about eliminating clutter or lightening a room; it was about beginning to work with her home. I told her that I could show her where to begin. It might feel challenging at first, but her home would love her for it.

No two beginnings are the same. We have different homes and our problems are personal. Even so, I have found that there are two general starting points that correspond to two general types of people. As you think about getting started on your house project, give some thought to which of the two types—cool or warm—best describes your approach to your living environment.

Warm and Cool People

As many cool people as there are in the world, there are just as many warm people. One is not better or worse, more desirable or less desirable. They are simply different.

You typically hear about warm people. These are the ones who worry about clutter and organizing and who tend to obsess much more about their homes. They are often gregarious, friendly, and generous. Warm people are good hosts but are bad with cleaning and clutter. They are challenged by excessiveness and attachment to people and things.

Is this you?

Cool people use their homes less and often find them an inconvenience. They want them to be comfortable but keep them as low-maintenance as possible. Efficient by nature, cool people are often sharp, smart, and independent. Cool people are good guests, but they are not great at making things comfortable. Cool people are great at avoiding clutter. At home, they are not do-it-yourselfers, and they feel clumsy. They are challenged by not feeling attached enough to people and things.

Is this you?

Cool People: Diana

During a preliminary interview on the phone, Diana said, "My apartment makes me sad." She also said her apartment felt cold and that she wished it was warm and inviting, especially after a long day's work. She said that she wasn't sure whether she needed therapy or her apartment needed work, so Apartment Therapy seemed like the perfect solution to her.

Two days after our conversation, I met Diana at her apartment for our first appointment. An attractive professional in her late twenties, she lived in a beautiful one-bedroom apartment in the West Village. Upon opening her door to me, Diana immediately apologized for her apartment's messiness. Was it messy? Not really. Was it cold? A bit. Was she insecure about her home? Yes.

She began rattling off a long list of things she thought I should know about her apartment. The furniture all came from her mother's house and had sentimental value. She knew that she needed to paint. She never cooked. Should the large print be hung in the living room? she asked, looking at me with a worried expression. I couldn't get a word in edgewise.

"How do we do this?" she finally exclaimed, looking around her apartment with her hands up in the air.

I was standing in an apartment three times the size of my own 250-square-foot apartment. It was prewar with low ceilings, original molding, and wood floors. There were large windows on two sides with views south and west. She even had a view of the Hudson River. To me, it had all the hallmarks of a stunning apartment.

I told her that I usually begin with a tour. I asked her to take me through the apartment, telling me everything that she liked and disliked about it, one room at a time.

"Well, that won't take long. It is very small," she replied.

What I saw as I walked through the apartment confirmed what I had suspected from our initial conversation. Diana was a "cool" person, and the hallmark of this was that she had a beautiful apartment that was barely lived in. It was sparsely furnished and badly lit, the windows were bare, and there was no food in the kitchen aside from mineral water, a gift box of champagne, and some expired vitamins.

As I walked around the room, I put my hand on the walls and was surprised to feel how cold they were. They could only get cold from the air outside. I asked her if she ever left her windows open. "Oh, yes, I like to keep the windows open when I smoke and then when I am out, because I hate the smell that the cigarettes leave."

With a continual chill in the walls, the apartment would always feel cold long after the air in each room heated up. Among other things, we needed to solve Diana's guilty feelings about smoking at home without freezing out her apartment. A good air purifier would get rid of the smell and would relieve her anxiety.

I asked her to put her own hand on the wall to feel its chill. She too was surprised by its iciness. "We're going to figure out a way to close your windows and warm these walls," I told her. "This is where we are going to begin."

Warm People: Carl and Julia

Carl and Julia used their apartment a lot. Carl was self-employed and often worked from home, a place he loved. Julia worked in an office but liked coming home in the evening. They had filled their home with beautiful books, artwork, and antiques, each with its own sentimental story. Friends and family came over often because their home was cheery and inviting.

So what was the problem?

Julia wanted it to feel more relaxing; Carl wanted to find a way to arrange his office. At first, the problems seemed very general. But there was a nagging feeling that they couldn't quite pinpoint.

When pressed, Julia admitted that she didn't feel in control of their home and said that Carl's office had taken over. He acknowledged that the apartment had gotten a little cluttered, and together they wished it were calmer and more organized. With good files, he could pack up his office each night.

On the tour, I found much more. Next to the bed was a tall pile of magazines stretching back several months, and days' worth of water glasses. There were objects under the couch that had been missing for months. They admitted that they should hire a cleaning person, but they just hadn't gotten around to it.

Pulling up their mattress to reveal the floor under their bed, I found a fleet of dust bunnies that looked like they could crawl. Carl had never seen these before. Julia had and was embarrassed.

Although we had discussed other problems, in every room I could see that cleanliness—or lack of it—was a key issue. While it wasn't out of control and things looked good, the growing dust and clutter of a heavily used home underlined every concern they had mentioned in the interview. Out of sight but hardly out of mind, the disarray explained the agitation expressed in everything they had said.

As we exited the bedroom, I asked them where their vacuum was. "In the hall closet, I think," Carl replied. Regardless of the need for files, I told them, a deep cleaning was where we would begin.

Whichever type you identify with, the cure is balance. Whether warm or cool, you never want to change your basic temperament. It is who you are and it contains your strengths. Therefore, warm people achieve balance by "weeding," since they have too much growing. Small things like cleaning out a closet, canceling a magazine subscription, or taking a load of clothes to the Salvation Army provide balance. Cool people achieve it by "watering and feeding," since they don't have enough growing. Their small tasks are buying flowers each week for the kitchen table, hanging curtains, and inviting a few friends over for a drink now and then. Both types should start slowly— a little bit goes a long way.

I am a warm person. I learned this more than ten years ago when Marre, my next-door neighbor, walked into my first apartment in New York City's Little Italy and told me I had too much stuff. Knowing she was a furniture designer, I had invited her over to show off some new shelves I had built. Instead of being impressed with my shelves, she said, "Why do you have so many things in your apartment?"

I was embarrassed. In my view, her apartment was minimal and Spartan. I felt that she just didn't understand me. I told her that I didn't have too much, that I had everything I needed and it was all carefully arranged. My apartment resembled a ship where everything was tucked into place.

"You have no empty space," she pointed out. "I can tell that when you do have an empty space, you fill it. Why?"

This was true. I considered any open space an opportunity for inserting something useful. I had built shelves in an old doorway, created a pulley system for my computer screen that lifted it up to the ceiling, and managed to insert a large drafting table into one corner, which I used as my second desk. I was very good at finding a use for any space.

"Why don't you take some things out and open up the space? It would look much better if you did."

What? Take something out? I thought this would be a death blow. Everything I owned was a prized possession. I had long considered my use of space an achievement and liked how everything worked perfectly. But I was forced to reconsider.

Marre's apartment, despite its severity, had a calmness and openness to it that my apartment lacked. Her apartment was smaller and yet it felt bigger. It was comfortable to sit in Marre's kitchen, and people naturally gravitated to her apartment to talk. She was right. My apartment wasn't carefully arranged, it was packed. There was no breathing room. It may have seemed functional, but it was crowded and required a lot of attention.

My life at the time was the same. I was struggling to write a master's thesis, feeling no momentum or excitement about it, and my relationship with my girlfriend was languishing. Working on my apartment seemed, on the surface, to be a healthy form of procrastination, but after considering Marre's comments, I started to see all of this activity as a big, warm security blanket. My home was my protection, my pacifier, and it was doing a good job. My life lacked movement and energy. With Marre's words, something clicked.

I began to experiment with removing objects from my apartment. I got rid of a chair. I took out the drafting table. I threw out a pile of old, mismatched dishes and mugs. What began as a trickle turned into a torrent, and over the next few months I emptied half of my apartment. As I did this my work habits changed, and the energy that I had previously put into creating and maintaining my home redirected itself into my work. I finished my thesis feeling good about it. Soon after, my relationship came to an amicable end, and we were both relieved.

Why Therapy?

Most people who are dissatisfied with their homes don't realize where the problems really lie. As in my experience with my old apartment in Little Italy, it is very hard to get perspective on problems that are right under your nose. Homes are tremendously personal spaces that don't lend themselves easily to clear vision. This is why I refer to my work as Apartment Therapy: when you work on your home, you are working on yourself, and when you change your home, you are changing yourself.

But be prepared! There is a reason why your apartment is the way it is. The home you live in contains a lot more than your belongings; it contains old energy and emotions that will be stirred up, which may surprise you if you are not prepared. One client, Amelia, delved into a drawer of photographs that had never been organized and found pictures of her old boyfriend, with whom she had had a painful breakup. With the tears and self-doubt that flooded the room for the next two hours, I was sure our project was over. Opening this box at that particular time in the project was a mistake. I have since learned not only to prepare clients for bumps like this, but also how to avoid the worst pitfalls.

One way to be successful is to know what to expect. Whether you are a warm or cool person, if you are unhappy with your home it is usually because the energy inside is blocked. When you go about opening it up, there will be a period where all of this stuck energy loosens and flows, stirring up all kinds of emotions. This can be highly unpleasant. You may find yourself thinking, "I can't do this—I am making things worse," or "This is going to be too expensive, and I don't deserve it." Then there is the urge for flight: "This is too much work; it would be easier just to move." Don't listen to any of it!

With the right coaching, the lethargy that surrounds this type of home improvement gives way to excitement and momentum. Big change is not impossible. It just takes patience.

Letting Go of the Past, Embracing the Future

Fifteen years ago my aunt Eleanor, at the age of sixty, told us she was preparing for her death. "Hold on!" I thought at the time. "What is this morbid plan and what is she up to?"

Strangely, this announcement did not have to do with the usual reasons: sickness, old age, or loneliness. It had to do with too many books.

Eleanor's library was remarkable. The biggest in the family, it was a combination of my grandmother's books and her own, which easily filled a hundred boxes. However, she had moved a number of times recently and had come to look on her most prized possession—her library—as her biggest burden. It was the heaviest thing she owned and the most expensive to move. After this last move, she decided it was too much. Holding on to all these books was doing more harm than good. It was time to give away her library.

Initially pained by the thought, Eleanor had come to see letting go of her books as an opportunity to come to terms with the first part of her life and prepare for the rest. She was not morbid about it; she was excited. She was eager to be free from all the weight and burden that she had created and carried around for her first sixty years.

First, she took out her most essential books, those that formed the DNA of her library. These she would keep. She limited herself to one box. Then she gave small selections to every member of our family before inviting close friends to come over and take a book for themselves. The rest of the collection was given to her local library.

Giving away the books was just the beginning. Eleanor also decided to clear away all the emotional clutter that involved friends and family. Over the next year, she had a number of intense and gratifying conversations with her children, ex-husband, and other family members. She also met with close friends and spoke truthfully with them. To finish, she straightened out her business affairs and sold off investments that had been languishing for some time.

Having made these changes, Eleanor found that her life entered a new phase. She was happier and more active than ever. Her discovery and the powerful act of giving away her possessions made me look at my life differently at a much younger age.

Today, I love books, but I keep my collection small and regularly work at editing my shelves. Due to my aunt, I learned that we don't need books as much as we need what is in them: their inspiration for the future.

Chapter Two

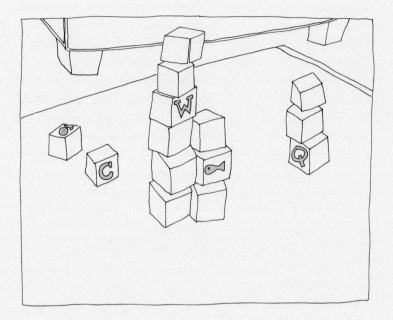

Seeing Your Home
in a New Light

Are you ready to take things out of
your apartment? Are you ready to invest time and money
in your home? Are you ready to let go of the old and
step into the new?

If you have read this far, the answer to each question
undoubtedly is yes. So let's get started.

In this section, we will shift our focus to the tremendous possibilities awaiting this kind of work, and I will challenge you to see your home in a new way by introducing two key concepts that I use with all my clients. The first is *flow*. The second is seeing your home as a body with four limbs: *bones, breath, heart,* and *head.*

In my youth, I found myself hanging out at the neighbors' house more than my own. The Callahans had a great kitchen, where everyone gathered on weekends. It was well lit, with a big table in the center and counters all around the sides. It was big enough for a crowd and cozy enough for a late-night beer when we were older. I don't remember spending many times like this in my own house. It was always nicer next door.

Everyone knows a home like this. Whether it's a small studio on the twenty-sixth floor of an apartment building or a ranch house in the suburbs, there are some homes that are more comfortable than others. It has nothing to do with how much the home cost or what part of town it is in. Some homes are just more comfortable. There is a secret to this.

What was so nice about the Callahans' kitchen? First, it was a well-maintained room. It was clean and comfortable to sit in, the fridge was well stocked, and meals were cooked regularly. It was a true "living" room, supporting the life that happened there. Second, it was well designed. In the middle were a table and chairs, and there were traffic areas on every side. The sink was under a window, and the triangle between the stove, sink, and refrigerator was easily navigable. Put together, the room had good flow. Movement, energy, and life made this kitchen comfortable and inspiring to all who spent time there.

Flow

The biggest secret to a beautiful, healthy home comes from understanding the principle that I call flow. Flow refers to the movement of energy through a space. It is a concept referred to with different words in Eastern practices such as feng shui or Vastu, as well as Western design approaches, all of which recognize that a space is most successful when it allows for full movement of energy within. While specifics among worldwide approaches to space differ, I have taken the general concept of flow as a unifying principle, and have found that it is readily understandable to clients and helps them see their home in a new light.

I first came to understand flow as a physical concept when I went to see a chiropractor for the first time after college. I was having severe back pain from sitting at work. What I learned from my chiropractor was a very simple and sensible explanation for the origin of my pain. The spine wants to move. It wants to be flexible, and when it doesn't move and flex it begins to lock up, which causes pain. Chiropractors generally work to restore movement to the spine; if this is not addressed, the pain grows worse, becoming bad posture, pinched nerves, and fused discs as the muscles tighten their hold on their frozen positions.

After the chiropractor had "adjusted" my back by moving it fully, I walked out of his office with a whole new feeling in my upper body, and no pain. I was stunned to realize a simple truth: that maintaining full and flexible movement is the key to good health.

When we are children, we are naturally inclined to move. Children run, talk, and express themselves a great deal, keeping their bodies limber and healthy. This is flow in its natural state. As we get older, there is a natural tendency to neglect this healthy movement and allow hardness to form. This clotted condition appears variously in our bodies as back pain, hardened arteries, and arthritis. In social groups it becomes stubbornness and dogmatism. And in our home it becomes clutter, blocked spaces, and dated style.

If your home is depressing you or stressing you out, it is undoubtedly due to poor movement and poor flow within your home. After working with clients and asking them many questions about how their apartments have evolved, I have found that after five years, every apartment begins to suffer from an unhealthy flow state if it has not been tended to all along. At this point, it can be a big job to restore proper flow. While many wait to address the issue, it is far better to take care of your space in an ongoing fashion, so that you never need to call for emergency help.

Flow: A Closer Look

Energy can flow in one of three ways: quickly, slowly, or not at all. In its natural state, energy flows slowly in a back-and-forth curving motion. This meandering motion can be easily observed in the movements of a snake, a flame (fire), a river (water), or a rising plume of smoke (air).

However, if you create a straight path, the energy flow cannot meander. Instead, it will speed up and move very quickly. The natural tendency to meander helps to slow the force of the energy down, as its course is constantly adjusted and its motion redirected. On the other hand, if there are too many curves or if there is no place to move, energy will slow until it stops and stagnates.

We see this very clearly in rivers. A healthy river will

straight = too fast

curved = too slow

meander = just right

always flow in the same way: with slow, meandering curves and straight lines. You can see this if you look at satellite photographs of the Mississippi or any great river; they create great long squiggles when seen from above.

Where a river is healthy, the water flows in a way that is peaceful and inviting to those on its shore. Sometimes, however, a river runs too fast. This can happen if it rains too much or when the river's sides are straightened with concrete by engineers. In these cases, the same river can become dangerous. At other times, a river can stop entirely. Either it dries up or a big bend separates from the main branch of the river and forms a pool. Along the Mississippi these stagnant pools are called oxbows. In both

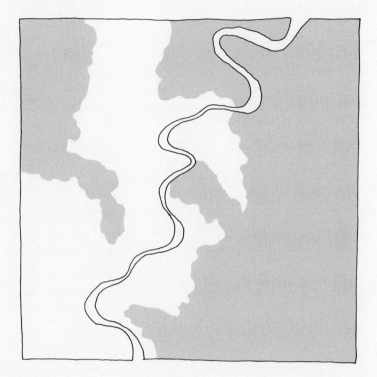

of these cases, what was once an inviting body of water becomes inhospitable.

Now consider your apartment. Imagine you open the door and let in a river of water. How will it flow? Will it rush right in and through your rooms, or will it get stuck and swirl around in dead corners? Ideally it should meander around your furniture, creating paths that allow the most movement possible throughout the whole room.

It should not, for example, run along one side of the room that is kept clear, while getting stuck and stagnating along the other side among furniture, clutter, and boxes.

Without thinking, most people instinctively tend to push things up against their walls and clear out the center of their

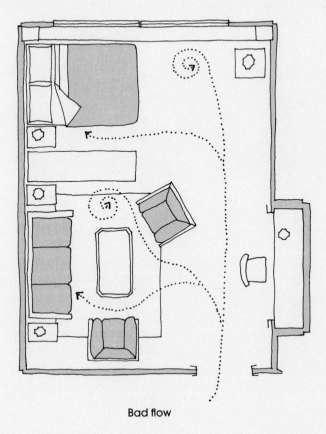

Bad flow

rooms over time. We do this in an effort to organize or "clear up," but we are only making matters worse. The resulting energy flow becomes wildly unbalanced, with fast, harmful energy running down the middle and dead, stagnant oxbows along the walls, where clutter easily forms.

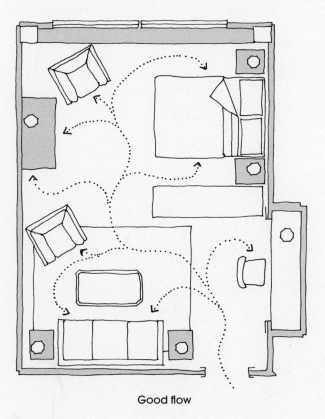

Good flow

Nora and John's Story

When I first spoke to Nora on the phone, she described the apartment she shared with her husband, John, as "cluttered and inefficient." Newly pregnant and thinking about the months ahead, she was "extremely stressed out" by her home and was having difficulty figuring out how to make it more comfortable. When I asked Nora what she liked about her apartment, her voice perked up as she told me that it was a beautiful top-floor loft in the West Village that got plenty of light.

When I arrived, I saw that Nora and John's large two-bedroom apartment was indeed beautiful. They had colorful, fun art on their walls and a big modular sofa in the living room, and their bedroom in the back was a quiet refuge.

But Nora wasn't wrong. Despite its good looks, her apartment suffered from a typical New York problem. Because it was a long and narrow loft space with a main room in the front and bedrooms in back, good flow was difficult to achieve.

Their main room combined everything—kitchen, living room, dining room, and entrance area—so they had done the natural thing and arranged their furniture all along one side of the room. The natural path from the front door through the apartment was a straight line, creating a bowling alley effect with rapid flow, while all along the other side of the room the flow was stagnant. As a result, they never found themselves using the front half of this room and were constantly struggling to keep it free of clutter.

Nora was right to feel uncomfortable about this room. As illustrated below, on the bowling alley side, the flow was too fast; on the other side, the energy was stagnating.

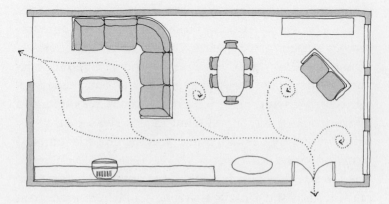

Flow along one side only

The Prescription

Nora and John were grappling with a very narrow room that needed to be rearranged in a way that would break up the alley along one side and redirect the flow throughout the space. This was my recommendation:

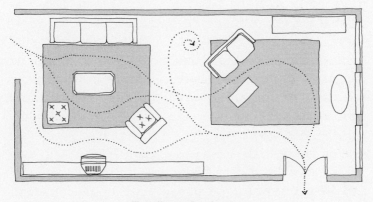

Flow throughout room

I took out the chairs and the dining room table and placed a smaller table under the windows at the end of the room. This took it off the wall and opened up the space. I then broke up the modular sofa. Although comfortable, the modular L-shaped sofa was killing the room, acting like a jetty and cutting off half of the room. It attracted everyone to one side, while the other side was neglected. I turned the love seat to face the windows and added a nice, soft rug and low table. This open space would now be inviting and comfortable for relaxing and working on the computer.

All of this made sense to Nora and John. They'd started out not knowing what was wrong with their apartment, but now it was clear, and they had a principle to work with should they ever move or want to arrange differently. The only tough part was giving up the modular sofa. This did not thrill them. After wrestling with the decision for some time, they decided to try it temporarily by putting a piece in the basement of their building. It never returned, and their front room took on a whole new life.

Seeing Your Home as a Body

I hear many different kinds of complaints from people about their homes. Some have to do with style and some with functionality, while others are more personal and subtle. Do any of these sound familiar?

"My furniture has no style or consistency."
"The lighting in the hallway is bad, but I don't know how to fix it."
"I never invite people over because there's not enough room."
"The clutter in my apartment makes me tense."
"My drain keeps clogging."
"I used to love my home office, but now it's grown into a rat's nest of cables."
"My apartment isn't finished. I don't know what to do next."
"I don't really like this coffee table, but it works fine. Should I get rid of it?"

Most people face a number of seemingly unrelated problems at the same time and don't know where to begin. Trying to tackle everything at once is overwhelming. It helps to recognize your home's troubles as symptoms and solve them separately.

To do this, think of your home in the same way you think of your body. See it as a living organism that grows strong with proper care and weak with neglect. By enlarging the concept of bodily health and applying it to your home, you will start to understand how your home can work better and see how to separate out and solve problems more effectively.

This becomes clearer when you realize that your home is made up of four parts: bones, breath, heart, and head.

1. *Bones*. The walls, floor, ceiling, windows, and fixtures in your home are its skeletal bones. With normal wear and tear, these basic elements break down.

Ailments: The sink leaks, the walls crack, the kitchen tiles come loose.

2. *Breath*. The way you arrange your home determines how it breathes. Healthy flow is blocked immediately by poor placement of furniture or over time by accumulation of clutter.

Ailments: The bookcases are too full; the mail piles up on the dining table; certain parts of your apartment are never used.

3. *Heart*. The heart of your home is expressed emotionally through its style: the colors, textures, shapes, and themes you choose. If the style of a home is unfocused or inconsistent, the home will lack energy, warmth, and pizzazz.

Ailments: The colors in the living room clash; the modern Italian sofa doesn't seem to fit with the Shaker rocking chair; the room is drab, with sandy beige colors predominating on the walls and furniture.

4. *Head*. The head of your home is expressed in its purpose—why you use it and what you do there—and seen in its design. A healthy home should support your activities. If the design of your home does not match your needs, it will lead to dysfunction and frustration.

Ailments: There is no good light to read in the living room; the kitchen drawers are not organized efficiently and you can't find anything; there is not enough seating for guests and yet you want to entertain more.

And along with those issues, there are others that most people don't relate directly to their homes:

"I am single and wish I was in a relationship."
"I am angry at my husband that we can't afford a bigger apartment. We have a baby on the way."
"I feel stuck in my job and want to find a more fulfilling path in life."
"There are things I want to do, but I never get to them because I am not organized enough."

These are the most important issues, and they often surface in the course of getting to know a client. Most of us experience personal frustrations like these at some point in our lives, and when we do, it is more than likely that they are manifesting in our home.

By curing your home at each level, you will be giving yourself a strong foundation to solve these deeper issues as well. As you look at each one, you will see that each builds on the previous part, with an obvious progression from the bones to the head. If you remember our original list of problems, you will now see that each one belongs to a specific area of your home.

Let's take a tour again, looking more closely at each limb as you would see it in your apartment.

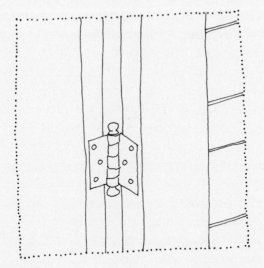

The Bones

The bones are the physical structure of your home. They form the vessel within which you live. It is very important that they are kept clean and in good condition or else they will harbor stagnant energy and transmit a dull feeling.

You have heard people talk about an apartment having "good bones," meaning that its basic structure is sound. Even apartments that seem on the surface to have blemishes can still have good bones. Underneath the unhealthy appearance the walls and ceilings are solid, the floors are in good shape, and the rooms are ample, with a layout intelligent enough to make for a very nice home.

Older apartments, such as prewar apartments in New York City, usually have better bones than newer ones. The proportions of the rooms are more generous and the quality with which they were built is often still evident in details such as the thickness of the wood floors and the hardware on the closets. These older apartments with their thick plaster walls are tough and respond well to renovations. They are akin to a hand-crafted antique chair, as opposed to a mass-produced Ikea product. They age well.

Whatever your situation, the bones of your home should be addressed first. Whether you are looking at an apartment for the first time or have already lived in one for a while, cracked tiles, worn wood floors, and windows that don't open easily are all repairs that need to be addressed right away.

Proper care of the bones requires regular cleaning. Consider this preventative medicine for your home, like brushing and flossing are for your teeth. In the same way that plaque builds up on teeth, so do dust, dirt, and grease in your home. It happens gradually, and if it is not attended to, you will be faced with a host of problems ranging from mildew-stained bathroom tiles to dusty surfaces and even bedbugs. Taken to the extreme, a lack of regular cleaning can result in health problems such as allergies and asthma. In the Eight-Week Cure, cleaning is an essential part of your weekly practice, and it should become a regular habit.

Finally, taking care of the bones is not simply about outward appearances. In feng shui, household dust is a major sign of stuck, depressed energy. On a very subtle level, the cleanliness of your home has a direct impact on your own energy and vitality. When I walk into a home that is cleaned regularly, I instantly sense a crispness and electricity in the air and find that the same liveliness is usually present within the owners themselves.

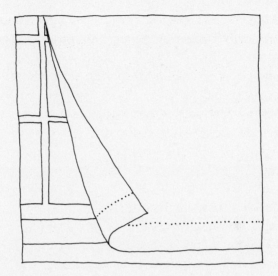

The Breath

Breath refers to the arrangement of your home. It describes the flow through each room and how you make space for each of the activities that you want to take place within them. The proper arrangement of furniture and removal of clutter support healthy breath in your home. This is what Nora and John were grappling with.

There are four things to look at when considering the breath:

1. How the rooms are sited
2. How the furniture is arranged
3. Where the lighting is placed
4. How books, clothes, and other collections are stored

When an apartment is empty, it is not yet alive. It is only when you move into it with all of your belongings that it begins to breathe with life. Proper arrangement and good storage then become crucial for healthy flow throughout. As with the river analogy earlier, how you arrange your front entrance, your living room, and your bedroom sets the breathing in motion and regulates it, either fast or slow. As with our own breathing, this level is unconscious, and after moving in many people don't think about how they arrange their space; it just happens.

The Heart

Beth had a beautiful one-bedroom apartment on Riverside Drive in the northern part of Manhattan. With windows facing the Hudson River and generously proportioned rooms, the apartment shouldn't have been anything less than impressive, but it wasn't. When Beth called me, she said her apartment felt "unfinished" and "blah." She had moved in five years earlier and had all the furniture she needed, but something was wrong. When we got to talking, an interesting story came out.

When she moved in, she'd been single and hadn't cared too much about her apartment. In this way, Beth was a typical cool person. Now she felt differently. She had been buying colorful clothes for the past year and her whole wardrobe was changing. Now she wanted her home to be more colorful, *and* she wanted it to be finished.

Beth was also in love. She had just started dating a new man, and her emotions were beginning to flow again after a long dry spell. Compared to her emotional life, her apartment was stuck in the past. Though it had great bones and breath, it was a white box with beige furniture, light brown wood floors, and not much on the walls. There was no color anywhere. It had no heart.

Over the next two months, with colors and fabric inspired by her wardrobe, Beth systematically injected color throughout the apartment, starting with the floor, which she stained a dark mahogany. This grounded and warmed each room. The walls received coats of soft off-white paint that warmed them up considerably. She had the couch and chairs re-covered in bright colors that stood out against the off-white walls and dark floor. The apartment came to life.

As Beth put color into her home, she was feeding the heart flow in her life, and it continued to grow stronger and stronger. And that man she was dating? He would eventually become her husband.

The heart element is a tricky thing to define, because it refers to the emotional life of your home. When considering the heart of your home, the best way to understand and work with it is to first think about the elements that give it passion. Heart elements—color, shape, texture, and even scent—affect us immediately and consciously when we walk into a room. If an apartment is well arranged, it will be comfortable, but if it has these four heart elements, it can be beautiful as well.

A room stirs our emotions by leading our attention to a few strong elements, while the rest sit quietly in the background. Successful style is all about dramatic touches used sparingly. Most of the things that you have in a room should be practically unnoticed, while a few play a starring role, such as a vase of flowers, brightly colored lamp shades, or a commanding piece of art. If you have too many things jostling for attention, your home will be too busy and stimulated. If you don't have any, your home will lack pizzazz.

The Head

Bob and Jen called me because after nearly three years of living in their apartment, they were frustrated and unhappy. Jen said that they often didn't look forward to coming home.

On the face of it, they had a terrific one-bedroom apartment with lots of windows, right in the center of Greenwich

Village. However, they hadn't fixed up the apartment when they moved in, and the now twenty-year-old renovation done by the previous tenant left them with missing tiles in the bathroom, rough wood floors, and walls in need of a new coat of paint.

But there was also a deeper problem. The previous tenant had been an artist and designed the apartment to suit her lifestyle. She had done a very good job. It was bohemian, with some brightly colored walls, a built-in wraparound couch, and a shower with a view of the street. It also had a very small kitchen with little storage, because she didn't cook very often. Although Bob and Jen had completely different needs and a different style, the apartment hadn't changed a bit during their time there.

Bob and Jen joked with me about ghosts in their apartment, and it was true: they were living in an apartment that essentially was not theirs. Decorating and furnishing were not the problem; creating a space that supported their lifestyle was. Bob had no space to work on his own projects, and Jen, a teacher, found herself preparing for all of her classes in their bedroom. Both of them had personal work they cared about, but they couldn't do it very well at home.

With its doorless rooms, lack of storage, large fixed couch, and crazy bathroom, their apartment didn't support the concentration and focus they wanted; it supported the expansiveness and creativity of a single creative artist's life. This space needed to be more practical.

The head refers to the purpose of your home. It describes the reasoning behind each room and supports all of the activities that matter most to you. There are two things to look at when considering the head of a home: exactly what you do in your home and where you do it.

Being clear and honest with yourself about how you use your home will result in it having a strong sense of focus and purpose. Not being clear about the purpose for each area of your home will result in clutter and disappointment. If this goes on for too long, you will use your home less and less.

My favorite examples of well-thought-out homes are the White House in Washington, Hugh Hefner's Playboy Mansion in Chicago, and Ma and Pa Ingalls' little house on the prairie. In each case, what the owners care about and strive for is reflected in each and every room of the house, from the White House's majestic, white-pillared command station and Hefner's over-the-top pleasure palace to the Ingalls family's modest working home. While your style and goals may differ from each of these examples, your home should be no different in the clarity of its purpose.

Are You Ready?

So, are you ready to change your home and change yourself? Now that you understand that your home is much more than four walls and furniture, and you can start to see it as a living organism with bones, breath, heart, and head, it is time to get to work and improve it.

The following chapter introduces a plan designed to address your apartment's needs on every level. The Cure begins with an interview-style questionnaire and then keeps you on track as you take care of repairs (bones), rearrange (breath), redecorate (heart), and focus your space to suit your purposes (head). At the end of the book you'll find an ongoing maintenance calendar to keep your apartment in shape throughout the year.

part **two**

The Cure

Chapter Three

Listening to
Your Apartment

Nancy greeted me at the door and welcomed me into her home. A gracious host, she ushered me into her living room and invited me to take off my jacket and lay it down. "Anywhere is fine," she said. There were no hooks, no hangers, no closets within easy reach. This was the first clue.

"Would you like something to drink? Water? Soda?"

I placed my jacket and bag next to her couch and waited while she disappeared into the kitchen to get me some water. Looking around, I noticed that the light by the front door was out, and her coat and bag were in a heap on the couch in front of me.

"I am so glad you could come today," Nancy continued when she returned. "I am really sick of my apartment. This living room here is okay, but the two chairs over there are uncomfortable to sit in. They came from my parents, and they are really nice chairs, but you squoosh way down in them. I never sit in them. I mean, they look good, but I think I should replace them. And I'd like to know what you think about the artwork. This one over here is my sister's—I just put it up there. And this one, I don't know if it should go on this wall."

We hadn't even gotten to the room that Nancy had called me about, and yet the number of issues that were beginning to mount up in her mind was alarming. If she kept going, pretty soon we would both be overwhelmed, and I would feel the weight of Nancy's anxiety as well.

I jumped in as Nancy paused to catch her breath. "Let me tell you how I'd like to structure this. We are going to start with a tour, which begins at your front door and passes through every room in your apartment, returning to this point. We will go room by room. I want you to tell me what each room is for as well as what you like and dislike about it. I am going to listen. When we are done, we will sit down and I will ask you some questions."

"Okay," said Nancy, and I saw some of the anxiety pass from her face.

"Let's start here, in the entryway," I said, stepping up to the front door. "This is your first room."

"But it's not big enough to be a room!" she said, surprised.

"Of course it is. It's your hallway, and it's being overlooked. Whether we call it a hallway or an entryway, it is distinct from the rest of your apartment, and it's got some problems." I pointed to the dark light fixture.

"Oh. I guess I hadn't noticed that. . . ."

Problems that are right under your nose (or right over your head) are the hardest to see, and this is exactly where all home problems like to live. Taking a walking tour of your own apartment and sorting problems by the room they are in is a simple and effective first step.

Once we finished our loop and returned to the front door, I said, "Let's sit down now, and I will give you the Apartment Therapy interview."

"Great. Go ahead and have a seat on the couch." Nancy looked at her armchairs and then decided to pull up a chair from the kitchen. (Simply sitting down to a conversation with one other person is a challenge in many apartments.) "Do I need to write anything down?"

"Not at all. I will write everything down. I want you to forget all about your apartment for a moment. I am going to start off by asking you for your favorites in a number of categories. Who is your favorite actress?"

"My favorite actress?"

"Yes. Feel free to tell me the first name that comes to mind. You can give me up to three favorites or none at all."

"That's a hard question. Give me a moment." Finally Nancy said, "Well, I like Lauren Bacall and Katharine Hepburn."

"Good," I said, quietly watching her face and writing the names down.

"I used to like Meryl Streep, but not now. She is too Meryl Streep now, you know. And I love Emma Thompson!"

What Nancy told me revealed pieces of her inner style: the elegance and femininity of the older actresses, the passion and intelligence of the current ones.

The Interview

When I meet with clients I always start with a tour and ask a number of questions. As in therapy, an initial discussion is important. Giving yourself the space to step back, asking yourself key questions, and dreaming about what you really want out of your home is the best way to start this kind of project. With any important voyage, it is important to know where you are going before you leave the shore.

So we start with the interview. The entire exercise takes thirty minutes. I recommend that you go through the process of answering all the questions even if you don't think you're ready to commit to the program yet. At the very least you will get your wheels turning.

Find a quiet time when you won't be interrupted. Turn off the phone, the stereo, and the television. Sit in your living room or other main room of your apartment. Read through the following questions and answer them honestly. You may provide up to three answers for favorites and may leave a question blank if it doesn't apply to you.

Favorites

List your favorite in each category:
Actress:
Actor:
Artist:
Writer:
Music:
Restaurant:
Automobile:
Television show:
Clothing (designer or store):

How would you describe your style (3 words)?
1.
2.
3.

Personal History

Where have you lived?
Where you were born:
Where you grew up:
As an adult:

Whom would you consider a role model?

What three adjectives describe the qualities that you admire in this person?
1.
2.
3.

Apartment

What is the problem with your apartment (3 words)?
1.
2.
3.

If your apartment could speak, what would it say is the problem?

What one thing would you like to do or do more of in your apartment?

Eight weeks from now, when this project is done, if friends came to visit, how would you like them to describe your home (3 words)?
1.
2.
3.

These first questions sometimes throw people off. "What does this have to do with my home?" some ask. Inasmuch as you are the primary shaper of your own home, it has everything to do with it.

The process of listing your favorites can tell you a number of things, some of which are below:

Answering quickly = quick decision maker (need directing)

Answering slowly = extremely careful decision maker (need pushing)

Leaving blanks = weak sense of personal style (need to imitate)

Too many answers = want to fit a lot in, may have trouble with clutter (need editing)

Answers are very eclectic = style may not be focused or you may be conflicted about how you want to be perceived (need to be clarified)

Difficulty naming an artist or clothing = more analytical and less visually oriented (need to look at a lot of pictures to improve visual knowledge)

Additionally, you want to see if your own description of your style lines up with your favorites above. For example, Nancy answered the following:

Favorites:

Actress: Katharine Hepburn, Lauren Bacall, Meryl Streep,
   Emma Thompson
Actor: Gene Hackman, Sean Penn, Colin Firth
Artist: Isamu Noguchi, Mark Rothko
Writer: Richard Russo, John Steinbeck
Music: Ornella Vanoni, old 1960s Italian, Frank Sinatra,
   jazz, Frank Zappa
Restaurant: The Four Seasons, Elephant, Prune
Automobile: Audi A8 station wagon, old pickup truck
Clothing: Valentino evening gowns, Diesel straight-leg
   jeans
Style: Elegant, classic, comfortable

From spending formative time in Europe after college,
Nancy had accumulated a hybrid style that veered from
down-to-earth favorites like Meryl Streep, Colin Firth, a
pickup truck, and jeans to fairly high-end favorites like
Katharine Hepburn, Isamu Noguchi, The Four Seasons, and
Valentino evening gowns. She also had a lot of answers
for me, which, along with the fact that Nancy's style had
two strong poles, low-maintenance and high-end, told me
that she would need discipline and focus if her apartment
was going to be successful.

Here are her other answers:

Original Home to Present:

Born: New York
Grew up: New York
As an adult: Seattle, New Hampshire, Italy, New York

Role Model:

High school teacher: articulate, professional, dedicated
  mom, inspiring

What is the problem?

Too dark
No clear purpose
Too many dead spaces

What would your apartment say?

"I am tired of being let go. When will Nancy pay attention to me?"

What is lacking that you would like to do?

"Have guests spend the night in a guest room and have
  a desk where I can work."

How would you like this room to be described?

Inviting
Lived-in
Smart

Nancy had not moved around a great deal as a child but had traveled a lot as an adult. I could guess that having a stable, comfortable home was something she knew and would be good at working on. By comparison, people who moved many times as children often find it hard to build their own nest, as they never completely trust that they will be staying.

The next three questions were similarly edifying. Role models represent our aspirations, and Nancy aspired to be articulate, professional, and dedicated, which meant she wanted focus and passion in her life. Her apartment stood for how she felt about herself right now: a bit useless and without clear purpose or passion. Her final answers were restatements of what she wanted for herself, but they cast her into the future, when she would be much more relaxed. She and her apartment would be "inviting" (comfortable), "lived in" (experienced), and "smart" (intelligent, articulate, professional).

While Nancy's style was all over the place, her aspiration was extremely clear, and getting her house in order had a clear purpose. She wanted to get rid of "dead space," focus her energies, and find some momentum in her life. All of this would start with her home.

As you look over your own answers, consider two things: do your style choices (the favorites) all point in one direction, and are your aspirations clear? I find that most people do very well with their aspirations questions but have trouble with their style questions. However, it is the clarity of your aspirations that is most important.

Now let's look more closely at your apartment. The following quiz is one that I have created specifically for this book as a self-diagnostic. Read through the following sixteen questions and check the appropriate box on the right.

		yes	no

Head

1. Does your home support everything you want to do?
2. Do you use your home often?
3. Is there room for everything you want to do at home?
4. Is there a good space for what is most important to you?

Heart

5. Do you consider your home beautiful?
6. Do you feel you have a sense of style?
7. Does your clothing express your style?
8. Does your home express your style?

Breath

9. Do you consider your home comfortable?
10. Do you sleep well at night?
11. Is your apartment organized?
12. Is it easy to clean and declutter?

Bones

13. Do you consider your home to be in good shape?
14. Is everything in good working order?
15. Do you take care of repairs quickly?
16. Do you clean your home often?

Number of yes's divide by sixteen

FINAL SCORE

If your home is in perfect shape and your life well supported by it, you will have answered yes to all of the questions above. The question is how many times did you answer no, and in what areas? Were your no's limited to one area, or were they spread out around your home?

Add up the number of times you checked yes to find your score:

12–14:

Excellent health. Invigorating. Occasional updating and ongoing maintenance are all that is needed.

9–11:

Healthy. Comfortable. Could use improvement in at least one area and toning all around.

4–8:

Weak. Energy drain. Visible problems in need of work have probably been put off for some time.

0–3:

Very ill. Depressing. Serious problems that are harmful to your health.

The result of this quiz will tell you how much work you have to do in the weeks ahead. For those of you who have weak or ill homes, your work will be the most intense and your result the most dramatic. You should also consider enlisting help right away to provide more muscle and momentum and make the project run more smoothly. If your home is healthy or in excellent health, good for you! Your work will be to raise the bar and improve upon an already strong foundation.

We all usually have one area that nags at us the most. If this is true for you, make a note of it right now by circling that area in the quiz. When you begin the Cure, this is the area that you need to pay the most attention to.

How the Cure Is Organized

The complete Cure is divided up into eight weekly chapters. This is not a randomly chosen amount of time. It is just long enough to complete a sizable home improvement project and not so long that you lose focus and exhaust yourself. Eight weeks is also enough time within which to create strong new habits for the way you live at home. However, if you wish to advance more quickly and combine weeks, you should feel free to do so.

Each week of the Cure is also divided into two sections: Deep Treatment and One-Room Remedy. The first leads you through all the steps necessary for deeply revitalizing your home at minimal expense. The second is for those who are ready to transform one room of their home.

The Deep Treatment template is designed to cover a typical one-bedroom apartment, and you should stretch or abbreviate the template to match yours. The game plan for the Deep Treatment section looks like this:

Week One—Whole apartment: clean, list repairs
Week Two—Kitchen: clean, declutter, cook
Week Three—Front hall: clean, declutter, plan a
Landing Strip
Week Four—Living Room: clean, declutter, arrange
color
Week Five—Office: clean, declutter, organize office
Week Six—Bathroom: clean, declutter, arrange light
Week Seven—Bedroom: clean, declutter, arrange art
Week Eight—Whole apartment: get ready for a
housewarming

The One-Room Remedy section is designed to help you focus on one room in your apartment that is desperately sick or could use an update. You may use it to take on as big or small a project as you like. It involves making a budget, hiring help, and planning ahead. The game plan for accomplishing a project in eight weeks looks like this:

Week One—Plan: create vision and check budget

Week Two—Plan: develop floor plan and Shopping List

Week Three—Plan: research furniture and services

Week Four—Plan: interview and book contractor

Week Five—Work: choose colors, order from list, decide on contractor or self to do work

Week Six—Work: contractor or self to do work

Week Seven—Work: clean up and reinstall

Week Eight—Finish up: add final touches and preparation for house-warming

At this point you are ready to decide which path to take. If your home has scored eight or below on the quiz, you'll probably need to focus your time and energy on the Deep Treatment alone. If your home score is nine or above, you're ready to add the One-Room Remedy to your program.

Chapter Four

Week One:
Creating Your
Own Vision

"I hate the green in this room!"

Nancy had walked me into the second bedroom. I was face-to-face with four walls painted a Day-Glo lime green in varying-sized horizontal stripes.

"What happened here?" I asked.

"My old boyfriend and I painted this room together. It took so long to do that I just left it. I really want to change it now. It's horrible. I don't know what we were thinking."

"What do you want to do in this room?"

"I need a guest room and would really like to have space for an office the rest of the time."

"Good," I said. "Let's leave the green walls aside for a moment and talk about those plans. If you could do anything, what would your dream for this room be?"

Nancy had been looking slightly anxious about the green and the ex-boyfriend, but now she smiled, her expression totally changing.

"I saw a sofa in a store last month that was so beautiful I almost bought it on the spot. It was an antique, but with modern fabric, wooden legs, and rolled arms. I imagined it in this room with my desk over there and all my books against that wall. I would really like this room to be a cozy little study."

"Do you have a picture of any of this? Of the sofa, for instance? Or a desk idea?"

"No, but I could get one."

"Great! By next week, I want you to check out that sofa, see if it is still available, and find some pictures. Look through three home magazines and pull out pictures of rooms you like. We'll use all of this to pin down exactly what your cozy little study will look like."

"Just collect photographs? That sounds like fun."

Nancy had been constantly bothered by her green-striped room and the fact that it represented some poor choices, but now she was off on a much more positive track. While there were some problems to be solved and old issues to be dealt with, Nancy needed to spend some time dreaming up the solution if this project was really going to succeed. All successful journeys begin with a positive vision.

Week One: Deep Treatment

Bones
Make a complete list of repairs and solutions.
Vacuum and mop the floors.

Breath
Remove one item from your apartment and put it outside.

Heart
Buy fresh flowers.

Head
Sit for ten minutes in a part of your home that you never sit in.
Look into earth-friendly cleaning products.

Week One: One-Room Remedy

Choose one room.
Gather pictures of rooms you love.
Start a Style Tray.
Visit your favorite home store.
Set your budget.

Deep Treatment

Bones

Make a Complete List of Repairs and Solutions. Walk through your entire apartment this week and make a complete list of needed repairs. Look for chairs that need fixing, tiles that need replacing, and lights that need new bulbs or rewiring. Imagine you were going to buy this apartment and you were making a list of repairs for an imaginary owner to take care of before you moved in. If there is a drain that is clogged, include it. If a faucet constantly drips, write it down.

Repair Worksheet

Room	Repair	Solution	Finished
Porch	New screens	Charlie	
Kit.	New microwave	Charlie	
Kit	Repair floor	Charlie	
Porch	Repair door	Charlie	
Bath	Replace 3 floor tiles	Charlie	
Den	Paint	?	
Bath	Paint	?	
Down stairs	Refinish floors	?	
Kit. ceiling	Repair & paint	?	

Include all of these items on your Repair Worksheet. This is the first item for your project file. (Your project file will have three sheets. To help you, I have included a template for each one in the Appendix, which you can photocopy, and you can find the Apartment Therapy Project Worksheets at www.apartmenttherapy.com.)

A needed repair that hasn't been done is a deep injury to your apartment and must be healed. The life of this part of your home is largely unconscious, and it is easy to let undone repairs pile up. You may not address the problems, but you know they are there. Attending to them is like tying up loose ends or clearing clutter—it releases a tremendous amount of stuck energy.

Another reason major repairs often wait is because it takes some effort to find the right person for the job. This week is the week to do this research. When your list is completed with all repairs noted in one column, make a decision to do the required research on each one and enter into the next column what you have decided to do about it.

Vacuum and Mop the Floors. When you embark on renewing your home, it is important that you break the ice and get to know your apartment intimately. The best way to do this is to clean it. Vacuuming and mopping the floors will get you acquainted with every corner of your apartment as well as how well the flow is or is not working. When vacuuming your way around rooms, it should be easy to get in and around every piece of furniture. If you need to shift boxes, furniture, books, or anything to do a good job, go ahead and do it and make a mental note that these might have to find a better arrangement in the weeks to come. Note that some types of floors should not be wet. In these cases a dry dust mop such as a

Swiffer will do fine and will even allow you to get under and around furniture more easily.

Keeping dust down to a minimum is extremely important for the health of your living environment. Feng shui tells us that in addition to triggering allergies, dust is the fine remains of dead energy and its accumulation contributes to stagnation in your own life. If you remember, when working in Carl and Julia's apartment, I discovered that the most important room in their house, their bedroom, had dust bunnies inches tall on the floor under their bed. One of the main issues we were working on had to do with the fact that they were not sleeping very well. Despite the otherwise cheery exterior of their apartment, no one had cleaned under their bed for some time, partially due to the items they had stored under their bed. Take the time this week to check under and around all of the furniture in your apartment.

Having the right tools for cleaning is important, because you will do a better job and do it more willingly if something works well. Although their machines are expensive, **Miele** and **Dyson** make the best canister vacuums I know of, and **Euro-Vac** makes the **Shark** corded mini-vacuum, which is extremely small and powerful. When choosing mini-vacuums, stick with corded types (not rechargeable, as these lose power over time) and those that include HEPA filters to ensure you are not simply moving dust around. (Originally developed during World War II to prevent discharge of radioactive particles from nuclear reactor facility exhausts, HEPA filters remove a minimum of 99.97 percent of contaminants 0.3 microns in size or larger, which is a much higher standard than a typical air filter.)

Breath

Remove One Item from Your Apartment and Put It Outside. This week you are breaking the ice, and there is nothing that will do it better than experiencing your first giveaway. You will be called upon in the weeks ahead to sort through your apartment and eliminate unimportant, useless items, but you will experience the process of breaking attachment right now when you try to part with only one object.

Choose one item (the bigger the better) that you don't need or use but which still has value, and take it down to the street. Consider your building's trash collection and place the item where it can be seen and easily picked up by someone else. It is not important that it be taken, but by placing it in plain sight you are signaling that it has some value, and you are making an offering to the world for the health of your home.

This simple task can be one of the hardest to do at first, yet once done, it transfers energy and excitement to the whole process. If you wish to do this multiple times during the week, by all means go ahead and schedule trips to your local Goodwill or Salvation Army store. However, this week you are only required to give away one thing.

Overattachment to possessions is one of the most powerful habits that you will encounter during the Cure. While possessions can be useful, vital, valuable, and enjoyable, excessive emotional attachment to them is unhealthy and can throw off the balance between what you own and the space that you have to house it all. If you are a warm person, letting go of belongings may be extremely hard for you, and doing it here will remain a valuable experience that will continue to inform the entire Eight-Week Cure.

Heart

Buy Fresh Flowers. Buying fresh flowers each week is an affordable luxury that will instantly enliven and beautify your home. It also sets a standard for attention to detail that will inspire you each day on your return home.

As simple as it sounds, the act of buying flowers for your apartment holds great significance and will heal your apartment on many levels. As organic elements, flowers strengthen the bones and contribute to the breath of your apartment through humidifying and cleansing the air. Through their color, shape, and smell they contribute a living beauty that enlivens the senses and invigorates our vision. There is nothing created by man that compares to nature's own work. And because they are ephemeral, cut flowers are a gift of freshness and faith to oneself and one's home.

Typically one buys flowers for another, but it is particularly important that, whether you live alone or not, you view flowers as a gift to your home. This is the beginning of nurturing your home and taking care of it.

Since buying fresh flowers is a weekly ritual, find one day of the week when it is particularly convenient to do so and a flower shop or corner deli that offers a nice selection. In most cities there are many stores that sell very nice flowers at good prices, but some are usually fresher than others, so it is best to look around before you decide. One client told me that he always stops at the same store on the way home from his weekly psychotherapy appointment, therefore combining all his therapy in one day. Another found a terrific source for fresh flowers shipped by mail, **Calyx & Corolla** (www.calyxand corolla.com) because the flowers are fresher, and they last far longer and smell far better than anything she finds on the street (they are more expensive, however). Whatever you decide, feel free to keep it simple.

Head

Sit for Ten Minutes in a Part of Your Home That You Never Sit In. To shift your perspective and gain some insight into a room that is bothering you or that intrigues you, find a spot in one room that you have never sat in or possibly even passed through. Sit either on the floor or on a chair for ten minutes in silence without television, radio, or music (turn the phone off as well).

Most of us develop flow patterns within our apartments that are so strong that after some time we rarely stray from them. If not for cleaning, we might never set foot in many corners of our own home or see it from any other perspective. The lovely, fresh objectivity that you had on the day you moved in easily gets lost as furniture arrives and life moves on.

As you sit, look around the room and try to imagine what the room would look like empty. Recall what it was like when you first moved in. If you are easily able to do this, observe the part of the room that you like least and imagine taking away all the furniture from that part of the room. Now slowly bring it back, but only those elements that feel good. In this fashion, try to isolate what specific thing in this room doesn't work well for you. Make a note of it on your Interior Design Worksheet (see the Appendix).

Problems often loom large but are caused by very specific, small elements. This is true in life as well as in rooms. If you ever have an itch or an ache on your body and instead of touching it you close your eyes and direct all of your attention to that place on your skin where you feel the disturbance, you will find that pretty soon the area of the disturbance becomes smaller and smaller until it is coming from one tiny point. If you continue to concentrate on this point successfully, the disturbance will disappear entirely.

This exercise is not intended to make your interior problems disappear, but it will allow you to begin to isolate specific changes that you want to make, and steer past the anxiety of feeling a whole room needs to be changed.

Look into Earth-Friendly Cleaning Products. We use cleaning products in our homes every day, from body soaps to shampoos, from dish and laundry soaps to powerful floor and bathroom cleaners. Many of these common products are harmful to the environment and to our own health as well. However, there are now many natural cleaning products that do these jobs extremely well.

Earth-friendly products help give your apartment a healthier feel because they don't leave artificial lingering strong or chemical smells. In particular, I have found that the use of dish soap based on herbs instead of lemons or other acidic fruit is a far more pleasing and cooking-compatible scent in the kitchen. Additionally, the old-fashioned powder cleanser **Bon Ami** has proven itself a true cleaner for the ages, as its biodegradable, nontoxic composition and tough cleaning power make it the best of its class.

There is only one area that I have found that earth-friendly cleaning products don't do as well on, and that is the whitening of enamel on sinks and bathtubs. In this instance, I recommend a small bottle of a bleach cleanser such as **Softscrub** for occasional use. As soon as a good natural product is made that solves this problem, I'll use it instead.

Here are my favorites:
1. Dish soap: **Caldrea** with lavender
2. Laundry detergent: **Seventh Generation**
3. General floor cleaner: **Murphy's Oil Soap**

4. Surface powder: **Bon Ami**
5. Window cleaner: Vinegar and water
6. Bathroom cleaner: **Dr. Bronner's Sal Suds**

While I've listed a few favorite products above, in other categories, such as surface spray and toilet and shower cleaner, I recommend products from **Caldrea** and **Seventh Generation** as well as these other excellent companies: **Bio-Kleen, Ecover,** and **Method.**

All of these can be found online, and a number of them are readily available locally at stores like Whole Foods and many regular grocery stores. **Method** is now sold by the giant chain Target, which discounts the price considerably.

One-Room Remedy

Choose One Room. Knowing that you now will have the time and knowledge to change one room, choose which one it is to be this week. Depending on how ambitious you feel, you can choose a smaller or a larger room, but make sure that your choice will solve at least one of the three main problems you identified during the self-diagnosis. For example, if you are not sleeping well, choose your bedroom. If you want to cook more, select the kitchen. Choose a project that supports one of the goals for your home that you listed during the interview.

Gather Pictures of Rooms You Love. Once you have chosen a room, your first project is to let yourself dream. Forget the space you live in and create a vision of what you want. Do you want to live in a modern white pad or a cozy country retreat? Do you want your home to be colorful and funky or clean and austere? Allow yourself to think beyond what you already have. This will not only inspire you, but also motivate you to deal with the problems along the way and give you something to aim for.

Start with pictures. Pictures are the currency of design, and if you hire someone, you will need to express what you are after via pictures. Until you have a picture of what you want in your hands, it will be impossible to pin down anything.

In particular, when storage is a big issue, I find photographs of storage solutions extremely helpful. Looking through magazines for bookshelves, kitchen arrangements, and rack ideas will often change your idea of what you originally thought the solution would be and provide a clear image for a craftsperson to work with. In the same way that you can take a photograph of a haircut you like to the salon and have your stylist reproduce it, most cabinetmakers or carpenters will work from pictures that you give them.

Home Magazines

The first place to look for inspiration is in a home magazine. A home magazine is simply a magazine that has to do with homes. You are looking not only for rooms to copy, but rooms with ideas and a feeling you can imitate. If you like the lighting of one room but the color of the walls in another, keep pictures of both. Read through a bunch, tearing out pictures of all of the rooms or ideas that you love, until what you have in your hands matches the vision in your head.

A few of the ones that I have used with clients are *Architectural Digest, Elle Décor, Metropolitan Home, Martha Stewart Living, Dwell,* and *Oprah—At Home.*

If you have never bought one of these before, you will find that they are all quite different, so flip through them at your newsstand before paying.

Home Catalogs

Another place to look for inspiration is in catalogs. The expert styling that has gone into their pictures can be helpful. Try Crate & Barrel, Pottery Barn, Williams-Sonoma Home, Hold Everything, Design Within Reach, Restoration Hardware, and Ikea.

Home Books

If you want to get ambitious, check out the tremendous crop of books on interiors. These can be found in any large bookstore or library, and they are usually colorful coffee table books with themes that tie themselves to countries or styles, such as Morocco, Loft Living, or The Green House. While you won't want to tear pages out of books like these, it is a good investment to buy one you particularly like and bookmark pages that appeal to you.

Your Neighbors

Your neighbors are another good resource; have a look at what those around you have done in their homes. In apartment buildings, many people share the same floor plan, and some of my clients' biggest inspirations for rearranging their homes have come from visiting upstairs or next door. To record these ideas, take photographs.

As you search for pictures, keep in mind that you are looking for three things:

Head: rooms that house activities that inspire you

Heart: a distinct style or color palette that excites you

Breath: arrangements of space and storage that are calming to you

Don't worry if the rooms aren't perfect. Circle the parts you like, and place pictures together so that you can get an image of a general theme.

Start a Style Tray. Professional designers like to see everything they are working with in one place, so you should too. Building your own Style Tray not only will allow you to organize your project, but will keep you on course whenever you feel uncertain about your vision. Find or purchase a white or black serving tray. You are going to use it to hold all of your visual ideas. You can also use a file folder or pin images to a corkboard, but make sure that you have one central place for all of the visual images that inspire you and that you can see them all at once.

Your tray may contain a few photographs of beautiful rooms, chairs cut out of a catalog, lighting ideas, and a number of paint chips. Not all of these need to make it into your final plan. You can put anything into your Style Tray. Allow yourself to try different combinations, juggling color, style, and texture until you get a mix that feels just right. Take your time. Sleep on it. Allow yourself to dream.

Put your Style Tray to work—move elements around and see them next to one another. If you have competing ideas, keep them on different sides of your tray until you decide which to go with. If you are ever doing more than one room, have a different tray for each room.

Visit Your Favorite Home Store. As you begin to create a picture in your head of the home you want, it is good to inform yourself of what things look like in real life. There is no substitute for being able to touch and see colors, fabrics, and furniture in person. As you begin to think about what will amount to a translation process from picture to reality, a visit to your favorite store is a must.

Even if it is out of your league in terms of expense, visit your favorite home store this week. Make mental notes on the individual elements that are the same in this store as you are collecting in your photographs. These elements might be paint color, type of furniture, lighting, use of fabric, or creative organization. Whatever you find, add it to your Style Tray.

If no home store appeals to you, keep your eye out for a restaurant or hotel that does. In New York City many of our most impressive rooms are in hotels and restaurants, and these are fair game. One client, Renee, saw tiles she loved in a fancy sushi restaurant on Park Avenue South one night and went back during the day to ask the staff where the tiles had come from. She found them and the store that sold them. They went into her Style Tray, and then into the final bathroom plan.

Set Your Budget. Setting your budget early on is a big help; you will be clearer with yourself as well as with others about what you can afford. When you have thought through and are comfortable with how much you can spend on this project, write this number down at the top of your Shopping List (see the Appendix for Shopping List).

Don't be cheap with your home! Many people who are extravagant in other parts of their lives and spend money freely on restaurants, cars, or clothing are often extremely frugal when it comes to spending on their home. Your home comes first, and allocating a reasonable portion of your resources for its improvement is something you should be doing each year.

As you think about your budget consider the relative cost of these different project levels in a one-bedroom apartment:

Level I:	minor repair work	$100–300
Level II:	cleaning, rearranging, and decluttering	$150
Level III:	buying and installing a new light fixture	$350
Level IV:	installing a new carpet in one room	$800–$2,000
Level V:	painting a one-bedroom apartment (5 days)	$1,800–$2,500
Level VI:	purchasing a new living room sofa	$1,000–$5,000
Level VII:	installing custom bookcases	$4,000–$10,000
Level VIII:	redoing a small kitchen	$10,000–$25,000

Levels I and II are part of the Deep Treatment, while Levels III to VIII encompass interior projects that typically require the help of others. Given the costs associated with the higher levels, one can understand why such a premium is placed on Levels I and II. These levels have the most power at the lowest cost to directly refresh and increase the vitality of your home. However, with normal wear and tear and changes in lifestyle, most people need to work on the higher levels at least every seven to ten years.

If You Own

If you own your apartment, you will be mentally prepared to make a bigger investment. For a small annual
makeover, consider spending a sum comparable to one
month's mortgage payment or what the rent on your apartment would be if you rented it. Of course, mortgages and
rents can differ widely, but it will help if you consider
that you are investing roughly one-twelfth of the annual
cost of your apartment in the interior each year. So if your
monthly housing bill is $3,000, this is what you should
spend each year on the interior.

For larger, onetime projects, such as when you move
in or hit the seven-year mark, consider spending as much
as you would on an automobile. This practice came from
a client who told me that her budget was going to be
exactly what she would be spending on a car if she had
one (she didn't, being a New Yorker). The logic here is
that the amount you will spend on a car is an accurate,
personal number. It is closely linked to your style and
what you can generally afford. Thinking in terms of auto-
mobiles is a good way to look at those big moments
when you are moving in or redoing your home.

If You Rent

While rents and square footage can vary widely, I recommend investing at least two to three months' rent in
your home when you move in. And I wouldn't shy away
from putting some of this toward improvements in the
bones, which is typically the responsibility of the landlord. You may not own the apartment, but it is still your
home, and making it comfortable is to your advantage.
Don't hesitate to paint, replace a stove, or change light

fixtures if your landlord won't. That said, if you have a good relationship with your landlord (i.e., if you schmooze properly), they may pay half of any improvements that you make once they approve.

As far as a yearly investment in a rental home, one month's rent is more than enough to keep your home in tip-top shape.

Tips for setting your budget:

1. Consider the expense an investment in yourself.
2. Make a large investment every seven years (the amount you'd spend on a car).
3. Make a small investment each year (one-twelfth of the yearly value).
4. Address lowest-level problems first (i.e., repair the shower before re-covering the couch).
5. Concentrate your expenses in one room at a time (i.e., furnish one room, rather than using the same money to partly furnish two rooms).

Chapter Five

Week Two:
Clearing the Path

"I know there's a lot of stuff in here, but I don't have any other place for it," Andy told me.

"Have you considered going through it and getting rid of anything?"

"Sure. I've been through the place a number of times, but it's all important. For example, that chair and desk were my grandfather's, that chest fits my winter parka and ski clothes, I use the exercise bike every day, and I love my books."

Andy's new one-bedroom apartment was very small, and all of his possessions didn't fit in. Each of the three main rooms was crammed with excess belongings, and it wasn't relaxing or attractive.

"I know that with your help, we can find ways to store everything better," he said hopefully.

Many clients want to be able to fit everything in, but even when it is possible, this is rarely a panacea.

"Andy, we will store things better, but as we work through each room, I want you to reconsider each object and put as much as possible into an Outbox."

"An Outbox? What's that?"

"That means that we are going to designate a space— say, the corner over there—where we will put things that aren't fitting in, working, or adding to the room."

"Will they be thrown out?"

"No. Everything we put in the Outbox will be looked at again after we have finished each room, and at that time we will figure out what to do with it. It may come back into the room or it may not."

"Where will it go if it leaves?"

"Wherever you decide. It may be given away, sold, or stored somewhere else if it is really worthwhile."

"You're not trying to trick me into throwing stuff out, are you?"

"Not at all. I only want you to see your apartment at its best and then decide how much you still want to fit into it."

As we worked through the living room, Andy was hesitant at first to put things in the Outbox, but when he saw that they were still sitting there at the end of the day and the rest of the room looked much better, he relaxed. By the third day, he was casually tossing things into the Outbox and moving quickly. He became far more decisive about "cutting someone from the team," as he put it, and eager for the space he was opening up. It still didn't change the fact that there were many things in the Outbox that he felt were important, but he knew we would deal with that later.

When he finally finished cleaning out his living room, the difference was clear. Among the things that Andy had put in the Outbox were the exercise bike, books, and his grandfather's desk and chair.

"I still think some of this stuff is important," Andy said. "I just don't want to live with it. Now what do we do?"

With the apartment looking a lot better and the full Outbox sitting in front of us without any drama hanging over it, we were able to easily decide what to do with each item. The bike was sold (Andy was going to join a gym near work instead), the desk and chair went back to his parents' house for the time being, and the rest was given away.

Weeks later, after the entire apartment was done, I saw Andy again. The first thing he told me was how much nicer his apartment was due to the rearranging and redecorating, but the last thing he said came in an embarrassed tone of voice: "I can't believe that I was living with all that junk."

Week Two: Deep Treatment

Bones
Fix one thing in your apartment yourself.

Clean your kitchen from top to bottom and throw away old food.

Buy a water filter and use it.

Breath

Run your hands over every wall in your apartment.
Clear space for an Outbox.
Clear one surface and use the Outbox.

Heart

Buy fresh flowers.
Determine your style.

Head

Find a new recipe and cook one meal at home.
Choose the date for your housewarming.

Week Two: One-Room Remedy

Decide what activities you want in your room and where
they will go.
Buy, borrow, or make a floor plan tool.
Map out the room that bothers you most and work out
your solution.
Name your vision.
Build a Shopping List.

Deep Treatment

Bones

Fix One Thing in Your Apartment Yourself. Drawing
from the list that you have made, choose one object needing repair that you can personally "heal" with your own
hands. Do not choose something that requires a specialist
or involves some skill you simply don't have. There are

many small repairs that only require gluing, sewing, or re-screwing, and these are the types you should choose.

Do a good job. The point of this is not only to get something fixed; it is to get your energy into the bones of your home. Participation is like an electric charge, and by taking the time to pay attention and heal one small part of your home, it will be revitalized.

Clean Your Kitchen from Top to Bottom and Throw Away Old Food. This can be a big job, so tackle this on the weekend or spread it out over a few nights.

1. Clean all surfaces, inside and out, with a good earth-friendly surface cleaner
    a. Counters
    b. Cabinets
    c. Refrigerator
    d. Floor (if it needs it again)
    e. Stove
    f. Other appliances

Remove shelf liner (if you have it in place already) and replace, or wash and replace. Moving everything in order to do the washing will allow you to reach bottles, jars, and boxes that you may not have seen in a long time.

2. Remove all food
    a. Past its expiration date
    b. Unused for more than twelve months
    c. In containers that are nearly empty
    d. Of which you have doubles (combine if possible)

Clean up and get rid of food clutter. The foods we have in our kitchens should be fresh and replenished frequently.

Due to the tremendous amount of preserved and pack-
aged food and our tendency to overconsume, most kitchens
store much more food than they use. I have found that
certain items, such as canned food, condiments, dried food,
and oils, can sit on kitchen shelves for many years and
only finally be tossed out when the owner moves. Look
hard at your own kitchen. If a food item is old, throw it
away; if it is unopened and you will never eat it, give it
away. Aim to reduce the mass of your stored foods by
at least 25 percent.

3. Remove all cups, glasses, and dishes that are
    a. Chipped, stained, or unmatching
    b. Extra or unused

Many people have an everyday set of dishware and another set for special occasions. Everyday sets usually turn
into a hodgepodge of odds and ends over time, with a
growing collection of orphaned mugs taking up precious
shelf space along with Tupperware containers, chopsticks
from takeout, and portable coffee mugs. Seriously edit this.
Your goal is to have one matching set of everyday dishes
(eight to twelve place settings, less for small apartments)
and nothing more (save a fancy set if you have one).

Additionally, if your set is short a few glasses or plates,
make a note on your Repair Worksheet to replace them.
If your whole cabinet is mismatched, treat yourself to a
new everyday set. They are not expensive and your
kitchen will thank you for it.

4. Remove cookware you don't use

Buy a Water Filter and Use It. The tap water in our
major cities varies, but nowhere is it perfect. Given the

tremendous journey most tap water must make, through miles of pipe and complicated routing beneath our cities, the pristine quality with which it was delivered from nature is lost. According to Dr. Andrew Weil's book *Eight Weeks to Optimum Health,* urban tap water now is often loaded with fluoride and chlorine or contaminated with cancer-causing chemicals such as arsenic, radon, and trihalomethanes (THMs). Common microorganisms such as cryptosporidium and giardia also easily find their way into our water supply. Dr. Weil has written eloquently and in depth about the poor state of our water supply not only in cities but in rural areas as well, and I recommend his book as a starting point for those who are interested. As a solution, I recommend looking into water filters and purchasing one that installs under the counter, is tap-mounted, or works with a pitcher.

I have used the **Brita** and **PUR** tap-mounted versions for years and been very happy with both of them. These are easy to use and affordable, and they noticeably improve the taste of our water, whether we are drinking it from a glass or using it for coffee or tea.

Breath

Run Your Hands Over Every Wall in Your Apartment. This is a fun activity that people never do. Unless you have painted your apartment yourself, you have probably not touched every wall in your own home, and even then it was not your hands that did the touching. Moving furniture away from your walls, start at the front door and slowly walk your way around each room of your apartment, feeling the walls with your hands.

This is an observation exercise that will bring you into intimate contact with the bones of your apartment. Imagine your hands are placed against the side of a giant whale, and as you move, you are feeling the living, breathing skin on a much greater being. This is your home.

One trip around can take you half an hour, and you will learn things you never knew about your home: which walls are hot, which are cold, where there are drafts, where it gets dirty, whether your walls are plaster or drywall (plaster is solid and cooler, and drywall is hollow and warmer to the touch). By coming to know the physical structure better, you will be alerted to things that would improve it, as well as find new ideas for arranging each room.

You will remember Diana, whom I mentioned earlier. She was the one who told me that her apartment was cold. After our interview, I walked the perimeter of her apartment and felt the walls. In the living room the walls were extremely cold. When I mentioned this, Diana admitted that she kept her windows open during the day, when she was away, to clear the room of cigarette smoke. To solve this problem, we bought her a very good air purifier and were then able to keep the windows closed. I would never have known to suggest this if I hadn't taken the time to feel the walls of her apartment.

Clear Space for an Outbox. The Outbox is your ally as you proceed to remove clutter from your home. It works because it uses a two-step process that allows you to figure out if you need something without having to decide what to do with it immediately.

Most clutter clearers will tell you to sort through your belongings and remove a certain amount to the garbage, to recycling, or to a giveaway pile. This is a first-generation clutter-clearing approach. It focuses mainly on identifying clutter that will immediately be taken away. The problem with first-generation thinking is that it doesn't take into account that there are two problems: how to sort out the clutter and how to detach from individual items. Separation anxiety is the far bigger problem.

When faced with two anxiety-provoking decisions—where something should go (its value to the world) and whether one can separate from it (its value to the owner)—most people get stuck and simply hold on to things as a default. Second-generation clutter management unhitches these two stressful decisions. It deals with separation first and decides how and where to get clutter out of your apartment later.

Choose a space that is clearly defined. This area should be out of the way of daily activities and be a place you can comfortably allow to get messy and chaotic. A closet or guest room is perfect for this, but any small area or corner near your front door will do. Designate this as your Outbox. The Outbox is not the garbage, nor does it need to be an actual box; it is a halfway house for your clutter, where things go to sit while their fate is being decided. You should never be afraid to put something in the Outbox (and to encourage you, I have included in the Appendix a sign to be taped above your Outbox).

Once an item has sat in the Outbox for some time, it releases its hold over the owner and becomes just an ordinary object that one can easily decide what to do with. One client compared it to the phenomenon children experience when they fall in love with a rock that is wet or under water. Later, when the rock has dried off and is no longer shiny, it becomes just a plain old rock again, and the child's attachment to it suddenly lessens.

As simple a concept as it is, the Outbox has proven to be extremely successful in allowing people to clear out and heal their homes efficiently on a regular basis. During the next seven weeks use your Outbox and empty it at the end of each week. Here are the basic rules:

1. Anything can go in the Outbox.
2. The Outbox is allowed to be messy.
3. Everything must stay in the Outbox for at least one week.
4. After that time you have several choices:
   a. Take anything back out.
   b. Leave anything you are undecided about for one more week.
   c. Dispose of the rest by moving it to the garbage, recycling bin, or giveaway pile.

Once people get used to separating from their possessions first and disposing of them later, they tend to want to put more and more in the Outbox, and the process of clearing becomes quick and easy.

Clear One Surface and Use the Outbox. Now is your first opportunity to use your Outbox. Starting small, choose one surface, either a bookshelf or a dresser top or a kitchen counter, and try clearing it by letting go of as much as you can. These are the questions you should be asking yourself:

1. Do I use it?
2. Do I love it?
3. Does my apartment need it?

If your answer to any of these questions is no, place it in the Outbox. You will be able to revisit your Outbox at the end of the week and see if anything has changed.

Heart

Buy Fresh Flowers. Continue buying fresh flowers for your apartment this week. Depending on the freshness of what you find, your flowers may last longer than a week.

Refreshing the water in their vase and cutting and rinsing the stems will usually prolong their life. However, don't let this stop you from buying fresh ones. If last week's still has a little life left, give the stems a severe haircut, thin out the blossoms, and place them in the bathroom.

Determine Your Style. Now is the moment to determine your style. Whether you are going to be doing any refurnishing or not, knowing your style is extremely helpful. If you are taking on the One-Room Remedy, the goal here is to be focused and consistent. If you are more expert with style, you can feel free to be more adventurous, but generally I recommend that you try to match one of the major styles.

STYLE 101

Style is the combination of shape, pattern, texture, and color in furnishings that expresses the emotional and intellectual ideas of a past or present period in time. For this reason, style is extremely subjective, and all of us have our own favorites. Whatever style you prefer, all will work best if you stick to it. Consistency is the goal. Style sets a mood, and you don't want to mix moods in the same room.

For example, if you plan a warm, traditional living room centering on a couch with big rolled arms, it doesn't make much sense to buy a bright orange cube chair from a modern design store, no matter how cool the chair is. Be consistent. If you want variety, you can have it in another room.

To stay consistent, it helps to know what your style is, or at least what name it goes by. The first step is easy: a person's style is generally either Traditional or Modern. Traditional style references previous centuries, when hand-crafting was standard. Modern style began in the twentieth century with the advent of mass production and is defined by references to the industrial process. If it helps, think of Martha Stewart as traditional and Calvin Klein as modern. If you lean toward the Traditional, you will probably be drawn to a style that is associated with a certain part of the world. If you lean toward Modern, you will find yourself drawn to a style that represents one of the major trends since the Second World War.

Here are a few of the most popular styles:

1. Traditional
   a. English
   b. French
   c. World (African, Indian, Asian)
   d. American
      i. Country
      ii. Mission
      iii. Shaker

2. Modern
   a. Art Deco
   b. Bauhaus: original German leather and metal
   c. Midcentury Modern: Californian and Danish, molded plywood and prefab houses
   d. Retro Diner: Emeco chairs, '50s diner style

e. Mod: '60s–'70s pod style, groovy,
    curvaceous
f. Future Modern: clear materials, futuristic,
    space-age
g. Organic Modern: raw, natural, green,
    new Asian influence
h. Contemporary: an adaptation of all of
    the above, blended together, somewhat
    of a catchall

3. Eclectic: a mix of traditional and modern,
Eclectic is an interweaving of influences and often
leads to new styles. One form of this, Fab or
Directional, combines strong traditional shapes
with the bold mod and high contrast colors of the
Mod era. As of this writing, this style is just coming
into vogue.

Of all of these, Organic Modern has been very
much the style of the early 2000s. A little bit eclectic,
Organic Modern takes the simplicity and shape of
the Modern movement and mixes it with the simplicity and earthiness of traditional Asia, India, and
North Africa. Organic Modern ranges from the earthy
dark wenge wood of the W Hotels to a bright, orange-
walled interior with a clear Southern Hemisphere influence. In all of these interiors the simplicity sought
is not industrial but earth-oriented.

As you consider your preferences, narrow them down
to one style and stick with it. This will allow you to more
confidently make decisions about what to add and what
can fit in.

One client, Tom, wanted to finish a guest room that had only a bed in it. He could easily see that he needed two side tables, lamps, and a dresser, but he wasn't sure what would look right. After forming a Style Tray that included the bed frame (already in the room), he could much more easily see that his Organic Modern style wanted simple, dark wood shapes in the room. Working from the photographs in his Style Tray before doing anything else, he was able to focus his subsequent shopping trips and find what he wanted easily. Once he knew his style, there was no doubt his choices would work.

Head

Find a New Recipe and Cook One Meal at Home. Cooking and eating at home are central to the well-being of an apartment. Using your apartment for daily nourishment connects you to your food and your kitchen as well as your dining room, and spreads one of the best smells there is throughout your home. Using your kitchen regularly is also the only way to keep it in good shape. The longer food and utensils sit unused, the more the nutritive value of the food fades and the warmth of your kitchen recedes.

Start simply by finding a recipe that is not too difficult and that you would like to cook. Following, you will find a great roast chicken recipe to get you started. For other inspiring recipes visit The Kitchen at www. apartmenttherapy.com. Choose one day of this week to shop on your way home, cook, and have dinner by yourself or with others. This is not meant to be a dinner party, however. A simple, healthy meal is your goal here, fully using your kitchen from preparation through cleanup. Be sure to do all your dishes before retiring for the night.

Simple Roast Chicken

1 whole organic roasting chicken, 3–4 pounds
1 yellow onion, sliced ½ inch thick
A few sprigs of rosemary, thyme, or sage
Salt and pepper

1. Position rack in bottom third of oven and pre-heat to 425°.
2. Rinse chicken and pat dry, inside and out. A wet chicken will steam instead of roast.
3. Slip herb sprigs under the skin on top of the breast and place one inside the cavity.
4. Season with plenty of salt and pepper.
5. Cover and place in refrigerator up to 24 hours ahead of time. (The extended refrigeration is an optional step. You can also move directly to the roasting.)
6. Place onion slices on bottom of roasting pan and place chicken on top of onions, breast side down.
7. Fold wing tips under and tie legs together loosely with kitchen twine or unwaxed white dental floss.
8. Roast for 20 minutes.
9. Flip by putting a long fork in the cavity and gently turning the bird so as not to tear the skin.
10. Continue to roast until knife inserted in thickest part of thigh produces clear juices, or thermometer registers 180° (about an hour, depending on size of bird).

Serves 4 for dinner, 2 for dinner and lunch the next day, or 1 for dinner and several lunches this week.

Choose the Date for Your Housewarming. Though it is still the beginning of your Cure, choose a date now at the end of your eight weeks and plan to invite over some friends for a housewarming. This planning ahead is important. You need to be realistic about dates as you look at your calendar, and you want to get a day earmarked this week so that you are aware the clock is ticking. By having this party and inviting friends over to witness what you have done, you will ensure not only that you will give yourself proper credit for all that you have done, but that you will also finish the job.

When choosing a day, I recommend Thursday or Friday for a small cocktail party, and Friday or Saturday for a sit-down dinner. Earlier in the weekend is always best to ensure that your guests are fresh and looking forward to a night out.

One-Room Remedy

Decide What Activities You Want to Do in Your Home and Where They Will Take Place. In your self-diagnosis, you asked yourself whether there was room for everything you wanted to do at home. Look back at your answer now. This exercise will quickly highlight any issues with the room you are working on and give you a helpful overview of your home. On a separate piece of paper, write down the rooms that you have in your apartment.

1. Hallway
2. Kitchen
3. Living room
4. Bedroom
5. Bathroom

Now, in another column write down what rooms you would like to have in your home. Your list might look like this:

Have:	**Want:**
Hallway	Hallway
Kitchen	Kitchen
Living room	Living room
Dining room	Dining room
Bedroom	Bedroom
Bathroom	Bathroom
	Home office

If your list of existing areas matches up with the areas you would like to have, you are in good shape. But many people have more uses for their home than they have obvious room for. You need to make a decision as to where you are going to fit these additional areas if you haven't done so already.

Looking at the areas you have on the left, now "place" each of the rooms on the right into one of the existing rooms on the left by drawing a line to it like this:

Have:	**Want:**
Hallway ————————	Hallway
Kitchen ————————	Kitchen
Living room ⟍————	Living room
Dining room ——⟍——	Dining room
Bedroom ————————	Bedroom
Bathroom ————————	Bathroom
	Home office

In this case, you decided to put the home office and living room into the living room. If things are tight, you may have to improvise or take one thing out. For example, you might decide that it's more important to have a home office than a dining room.

The point of this exercise is to make clear commitments to each of your spaces. I have clients who regularly used their dining table as a home office and rarely used another room that was properly set up as an office. Having two office spaces and cluttering up their dining room with papers didn't work. They had to either recommit to using only their office or turn their dining room into a more functional office space, letting go of what it was intended for. They chose to transform their dining room, as they already ate dinner each night in the living room and were happy doing so. When working with limited space, you don't have to stick with tradition, but your use for each area should be clear and practical.

Here are a few tips on how to locate your rooms:

1. A hallway or some kind of entrance space is essential, so include this if you haven't already.
2. Avoid putting an office (computer, etc.) in your bedroom.
3. Once you have decided where an area is, collect everything that goes into it in that one space.

This last point is particularly important, because some people will let papers and books spread themselves around their apartment. This blurs boundaries between rooms and creates clutter. Keep your rooms focused.

Buy, Borrow, or Make a Floor Plan Tool. If you need to rearrange or plan a room from scratch, buy, borrow, or make a floor plan tool this week. A floor plan can be done on anything ranging from sheets of graph paper and a pencil to sophisticated computer programs.

When dealing with the intensely private space of your

own home, it helps to take an objective position and consider problems and solutions without stirring up all of the emotions living in each room. In much the same way that any professional relies on tools to help consider possibilities before trying them for real, the use of a floor plan tool is a tremendous aid in considering different options for a room without having to move a thing.

The simplest way to map out a floor plan is to use graph paper. Drawing the outline of your walls to scale on a graph is the first step, after which furniture can either be drawn on another piece of paper and cut out one by one, or simply drawn lightly into place. It is helpful if the furniture you cut out is shaded another color so that it will stand out against the room floor plan. For measurements of furniture that you do not have and are considering, you can find standard sizes in most catalogs. When choosing graph paper, I find that bigger squares and larger sizes of pads are easier to work with.

Another good method is a paper-based floor plan kit called the **Home Quick Planner,** which doesn't cost a great deal and will allow you to choose from a large range of standard furniture. It can be found at www. homeplanner.com.

If you like to work on the computer, there are two programs that I have used and recommend. They are Microsoft's **Visio** (www.visio.com) and **Smart Draw** (www.smartdraw.com), which are both simple and available for trial use for up to thirty days. Be warned, however, that Visio is extremely expensive ($500) should you ever want to purchase it, while Smart Draw Floor Plan Edition is more affordable ($198).

The benefit of using these programs is that your floor plan can easily be duplicated many times, allowing you to see different variations all at once. Additionally, your work can be exported to documents and sent via e-mail in moments. This can be helpful if you are working on your apartment with another person.

Map Out the Room That Bothers You Most and Work Out Your Solution. Start by sketching a simple line drawing of the room in question with marks for windows, doors, and openings. Be sure to draw in any fixtures such as radiators, half walls, or pipes that stick out into the room. Now use a tape measure to go around the room and measure each wall, window, and opening and write this down next to the corresponding lines in your sketch. Do the same with the major furniture in your room on another piece of paper.

Transfer this to your floor plan tool.

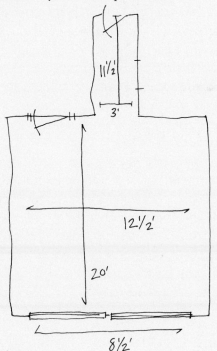

With the use of the room firmly in mind, begin to re-work your room as you would imagine it perfectly serving your purposes. Don't limit yourself. Imagine your ideal solution and then see if you can make this happen in your floor plan. View each room as you would if you were starting from scratch and had no limitations.

AVOID MOVIE THEATER AND
BOWLING ALLEY SYNDROMES

Movie Theater Syndrome

Living rooms usually have the worst flow. Since so many people watch television in their living room, far too often a couch is placed against one wall with the television on the other, leaving a big walkway right through the middle. Often there is one other lounge chair facing the television and a coffee table in the middle; it's where feet go when watching television.

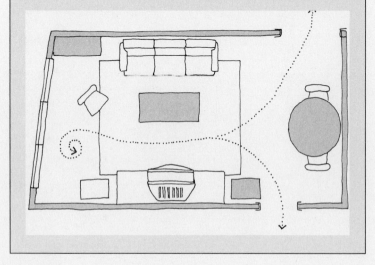

This is the "movie theater" syndrome. In a real movie theater, the intention is for everyone to face the movie and be silent. In a living room the intention should be that people will face one another and talk. Living rooms are the social centers of the home, and it is very important that, no matter where the television is, there be at least three seating positions creating a circle, allowing conversations to take place and stopping the room's flow from rushing straight down the middle.

Bowling Alley Syndrome

Another problem is the tendency to push all furniture up against the walls. This creates a "bowling alley" effect, with too fast a flow in the center of the room and a stagnant space on the side where belongings collect.

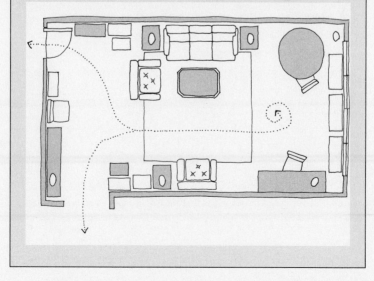

Here is a good test for these problems: without moving any furniture, are there parts of the room you couldn't reach with a vacuum cleaner? While some of the bigger objects like the sofa, shelving, and media cabinet might have to be placed against a wall (though not always), end tables, chairs, floor lamps, and other furniture should be kept at least six to twelve inches away from walls, giving everything a cushion of air around it so that good energy flow can continue.

Margaret's Living Room Becomes an Office

Margaret, a literary agent who worked from home, had a beautiful old two-bedroom apartment in Brooklyn. Her growing business put strain on her living space. Along with a collection of first-edition books that numbered in the hundreds, she was considering taking on an assistant and needed more space for this. Space, however, was tight, and the only room that made sense for her new, bigger office and library was the main room, which currently housed her living room and dining room. As we looked at this room on paper, we could see that it was big enough to accommodate many uses.

Realizing how crucial this move was for her business, Margaret decided that the living room could be scrapped and the dining area could shrink. Thinking big, we planned a long desk area along one entire side of the room, with plenty of shelving above for books and papers. With files below, there would be plenty of room for Margaret and her assistant to work at this one desk, and the entire room would take on the aspect of her professional headquarters. All of this was drawn out in the floor plan. With this picture in hand, it was easy to see how much needed to be taken out of the room, and determine measurements for what was to be brought in.

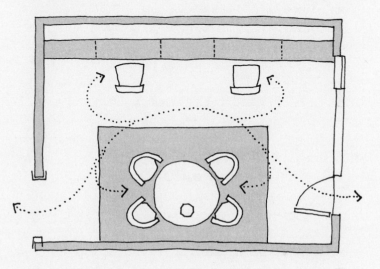

As you look at your room, refer to the following rules as you try different arrangements:

1. Furniture works best when centered on the middle of the room.
2. Couches and beds work best with tables and lights on either side of them.
3. Carpets should be big enough to either approach the legs of furniture or go at least halfway under it.
4. Keep flow lines shifting by allowing plenty of opportunities to go around furniture from all directions.

5. Place beds so that the foot points toward the door.
6. Place televisions and other media equipment on walls that will be the least visible from the room's entrance.
7. Move sofas off the wall whenever possible.
8. Don't block windows.
9. Always have at least three separate sitting positions in a living room.
10. Keep corners as open as possible.

When you feel you have hit upon a successful room arrangement, stand back and look at it. The design should be uncomplicated, so that it is immediately clear to any stranger exactly what it is used for. It should allow plenty of movement, and no area of the room should be inaccessible. It should be easy to clean. It should look comfortable.

Name Your Vision. Work on your Style Tray this week to the point where it includes ideas for everything you would like your room to be. If you need to gather more pictures and information, do so. If you have dramatically competing ideas in your tray, you should decide at this point which way you want to go.

Looking over what you have collected, come up with three words that describe the space you want. This is naming your vision. They can be any kind of words, and they should describe the style and feeling you are after. For example, one client chose "cozy, sculptural, inviting." Another picked "impressive, cool, fun." A third said she wanted "an exotic oasis." Write these down on your Shopping List (see Appendix).

MOVING MEDIA AND TELEPHONES

People often feel limited in their attempts to re-arrange rooms that contain computers, televisions, or telephones because they don't think that the wires and cables can be moved. This is not true, and you should feel free to find the right places for these corded items, as wires and cables are among the easiest things to move.

If your television has cable, your cable company can usually send someone out within three to four days to rewire a room; if you want to save money or get ambitious, you can do it yourself. Coaxial cable is just fat cable that you can buy cheaply in any Radio Shack or electrical supply store and connect to your existing outlet. It is easy to cut and easy to attach new fittings to, so you can run it wherever you want to. Telephone wire is even easier to work with, as all the pieces are made to snap together, and great lengths of wire are both inexpensive and readily available.

The real trick is hiding new wire as neatly as the servicepeople do it. For this all you need is one of **Arrow's heavy-duty staplers** (see www. arrowfasteners.com), which are made to easily fasten all different kinds of wire to your wall or baseboard. The standard stapler, which will take care of wire and cable, is called a **T-25 Fastener.**

Tina's Exotic Oasis

Tina had a small studio apartment on the Upper West Side of New York City and had recently bought a two-bedroom condominium in Florida, where she was able to spread out and spend time relaxing. Her New York apartment was therefore taking on the role of a pied-à-terre, which she wanted to become a luxurious refuge when working in the city. Her Style Tray was filled with photographs of rooms in North Africa that were saturated with deep color and had an exotic and tropical element to them. Meanwhile, her apartment was neglected, with a twin bed in the corner and a large air conditioner sitting in the middle of the room and currently in use as a coffee table. The beginnings of her exotic taste were evident only in small ways—in the lamps and a large dark wood screen she had placed against the wall. Tina described her apartment as "disorganized, messy, dirty: it makes me anxious." But she wanted it to feel "quiet, soft, serene: like an exotic oasis, a retreat."

Tina's vision called for paint and curtains to set the mood and create a separation between rooms. Investing in a larger bed to turn her main room into a luxurious bedroom was the best way to center the comfortable refuge. Despite Tina's anxiety, her Style Tray displayed a powerful and exciting vision. Everything we needed could be found within her collection of pictures, which included colors, fabrics, and lighting ideas.

Compare your Style Tray to your room. Is it similar to what you have or wildly different? Is it pointing you toward a refreshing of your home or a total makeover? If it is a change of style, does it require changing furniture or simply fabrics and paint?

Most people don't change their style, they emphasize it. Style Trays allow you to indulge yourself and locate your style safely. Once you've done this, translating this vision usually only requires editing out a few things and pushing what you already have further.

If you haven't done so already, now is the time to determine or define your style. Instructions for this are included in the Deep Treatment this week. When you have figured out your style, write the name of it at the top of the Shopping List.

Build a Shopping List. Now is the time to build your Shopping List using your floor plan and the ideas in your Style Tray. Taking the entire room into consideration, write down anything you need to buy, including furniture, light fixtures, paint, curtains, artwork, and so on. If you will need any service help, put this down too.

By writing down those things that you need to purchase, including services, and then affixing an estimated price to each one, you will be placing yourself in control of your spending and will be able to stay within your budget. Here is an example:

Amy's Shopping List

Amy and I spent nearly one month getting prices on everything for her bathroom renovation and the new shelves she wanted in her living room. She was extremely jittery about all the changes she was contemplating and how much money it would cost. She was afraid of spending too much and readily admitted that she was "neurotic" about the numbers. Amy worked at home, and the money she was contemplating spending, about $15,000, was a lot for her. Most of it was going to come out of a bank loan.

Part of the reason for Amy's insecurities related to her great difficulty focusing and staying organized. If something was uncertain, rather than pin it down she tended to melt down. The Shopping List process helped her to stay calm, and the process of gaining control meshed with her personality. After pricing out everything she wanted to do, we had a clear set of numbers for the whole project. The final price was over her budget; however, I knew we could now see where things could be trimmed to stay within it.

By spending a fraction of her budget, she now had a very important thing: information. Ironically, Amy didn't want to take anything out of her plan, so she decided to wait six months, save up some more money, and do it all. As she came to understand, having all of this information at her fingertips put her in charge of achieving her goals and did not leave her at the mercy of anyone else's numbers.

Room/Item	#	Description	Estimated Price
Living Room			
ottoman	1		$500
coffee table	1		$350
rug, 5x9	1		$750
floor lamps	2		$300
gallons paint	4		$100
days painter	2		$600
		subtotal (purchases only)	$2,600
		tax @ 8.625%	$224
		delivery	$200
		Incidentals @ 5%	$130
		Grand Total	**$3,154**

Prices

One of the trouble spots in planning makeovers is that people aren't familiar with prices. It can feel extremely risky to start a job and not know how much everything is going to cost, so you should begin to take the time after you have completed your Shopping List to familiarize yourself with prices.

For furniture, one way to calculate your expenditures is to flip through any catalogs you have that you feel represent your spending level and use their prices as estimates. For services, you will need to do a little legwork by asking your neighbors and friends, but you can use these amounts as average benchmarks in New York City:

1. Painter, one day $300
2. Carpenter, one day $400
3. Electrician, one visit $150–$250
4. Handyman, one day $200
5. Repainting, one-bedroom apartment $2,500

As you build your list you should also include amounts for tax and shipping fees. Tax in New York City is 8.625 percent, and shipping fees run from about $50 for an armchair or small table to about $200 for a large couch or bed. Of course, some companies ship for free, but it is much better to overestimate than underestimate at this point, as these extra fees can really add up when you are purchasing furniture.

I also advise putting in 5 percent of your total as an additional amount to cover incidentals. These are all the little things that you will need but may not anticipate at this time, such as paintbrushes, rug pads, or felt pads for the feet of new furniture. You will see a line for this on your Shopping List as well.

Chapter Six

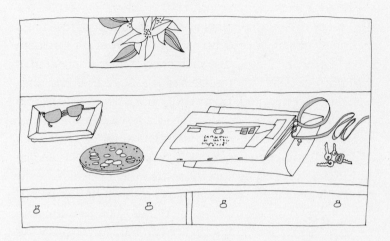

Week Three:
The Landing Strip

When I first spoke to Steven, his exact words to me were, "Can you help people with absolutely no taste?"

Not wanting to let him down, I said yes and asked him what the problem was.

"My wife and I moved to the city a year ago and our place is still unfinished. We just don't know how to match colors or fabrics or anything. At this point, we need someone who can tell us what to do."

After assuring Steven that he probably had more taste

than he thought, I arranged to meet him, his wife, Anne, and their six-month-old son at their home. When I arrived, Steven was a little late, so Anne offered me a drink and gave me a complete tour of their home. It was a nice two-bedroom apartment—a little sparsely furnished, perhaps, but not at all as bad as Steven had made it sound. When Steven arrived, we went through the apartment again, and they both told me a great deal about what was bothering them. They were very confident in their opinions, except when it came to style and color. In particular, they wanted help placing their rugs and choosing paint colors for the walls.

"We liked this rug, so we got three of them. They are all different colors. We put the bright one in the bedroom because it seemed warm to us. The others are out here in the living room. What do you think? Do they go?"

The rugs were lovely, but the colors they had chosen had nothing to do with one another or the rooms they were in. I was puzzled by their ability to recognize quality rugs in a store yet not know if they would fit into their home, but when I did the interview with them, I began to understand.

They had answers for all the favorites, except for a favorite visual artist. Their education and their careers were strongly weighted in favor of math and science. Steven worked in finance, and Anne ran the business office of a major magazine. While Steven and Anne were extremely bright and talented, I realized that they were not visual people and had not developed visual skills. They needed an easy way to think about colors.

"This is a beautiful rug you have chosen," I said, pointing to the biggest one in the living room. It was a closely striped rug with five different colors. "Do you see how many colors are in it?"

They both nodded. I could see that looking at colors in this detail was new for them, but they were following me.

"All of these colors have been chosen by an expert, a designer. As a result, they work well together. If you want to choose any other colors for this room, all you have to do is pick one of the rug's colors and apply it to other parts of the room."

"You mean that if we imitate this rug and stick to these five colors, we won't screw it up?"

"Exactly. For example, you can take this light color for the walls, this mossy green for the sofa, and this rich brown for the wood in a coffee or side table. No matter what you do, it will all work well together, because these colors were designed to go together."

"So we can use this rug as a guide. Can we use other things this way as well?"

"You sure can. Whenever you choose one thing that you love and use its colors as a guide, everything will work together nicely. This is a simple way to start, and it works. Choose one beautiful thing, study it, and let it guide your other choices."

"Got it. So we can use these three rugs to choose the colors for these rooms. What about the kitchen?"

"I really like the collection of colored bowls we got from your mother," said Anne. "We could use them to match paint colors."

Steven and Anne now had a tool they could use to make decisions. In keeping with their rational approach to life, Steven and Anne could now begin to decipher their visual style on their own. With this one meeting, they began to be released from the burden of believing they had no taste.

Week Three: Deep Treatment

Bones

Vacuum, dust, and mop (wet or dry) throughout your home.

Clean your entrance and any related closets.

Arrange to have all repairs taken care of in the next three weeks.

Breath

Declutter your entrance.

Move all old mail, catalogs, and magazines to the Outbox.

Look into what you would need to create a Landing Strip.

Cancel any unused subscriptions.

Heart

Identify cool rooms and warm rooms.

Apply the 80/20 color rule.

Head

Cook two meals at home this week.

Design an invitation for your housewarming.

Week Three: One-Room Remedy

Research your Shopping List.

Start a list of proposed interior changes.

Identify cool rooms and warm rooms.

Determine whether window treatments are necessary.

Apply the 80/20 color rule.

Research and call in help this week.

Deep Treatment

Bones

Vacuum, Dust, and Mop (Wet or Dry) Throughout Your Home. Repeat your cleaning of all floors and surfaces. This should happen every two weeks—more often if your home includes children or pets.

Clean Your Entrance and Any Related Closets. In one respect, kitchens are easier to clean than other rooms, in that they are usually self-contained and utensils and appliances rarely stray outside their boundaries, whereas other rooms are connected and overflow into one another. Even though we will work through your apartment in sections, once you begin moving things outside of your kitchen, a certain amount of disruption will creep into the apartment.

As you stand inside the entrance to your apartment, you may be facing a hallway, kitchen, or dining room. In many older apartments you will often have a small hallway and in newer ones sometimes none at all. Thoroughly clean this area and whatever space you use for your coat, bags, and spare change when you come through the door. Working from the surfaces to the floor to the closets, your job is to take everything out, wipe, scrub, or vacuum everything, and put back only what is necessary.

Arrange to Have All Repairs Taken Care of in the Next Three Weeks. You have already noted your repairs and found people or references to people who can help you with them. Next, you'll start to hire the people you need, making the necessary arrangements to have all repairs taken care of in the next three weeks.

Breath

Declutter Your Entrance. As you work your way through this area, remember this test:

1. Do I use it?
2. Do I love it?
3. Does my apartment need it?

Everything that doesn't pass the test goes in the Outbox, and you should be aiming to purge at least twenty-five percent of what you have in this area now. Be bold and give yourself more credit the more the Outbox grows.

As you approach surfaces you should be sorting through and getting rid of old mail, knickknacks, piles of change, old keys—all of the stuff that piles up around your doorway when you come in and empty your pockets.

As you approach closets you should be sorting through and getting rid of coats you don't wear, hats, umbrellas, shoes, tools, cleaning utensils, papers, storage boxes, empty boxes—all of the things that you tend to hide away in your front closets.

Collections

At this point you may be running into things such as handbags or hats that are part of a collection. Collections are full of character and they often represent a tremendous amount of effort, but they work against us if they do not have a proper home. I urge you to get your collection out of the closet and put it on display.

If you cannot easily put it on display, move it to the Outbox until you can assess whether there is room on your walls or on a shelf to show it off. If you love it, honor it; otherwise let it go.

Dan's Baseball Caps

A client, Dan, cared a great deal for his collection of baseball caps. Dan was extremely sloppy, so all of his caps were stuffed into his closet and hanging from hooks on the back of the door. His wife, Linda, considered them a nuisance. They fell off the hooks onto the floor, and Linda was tired of picking them up.

When I asked Dan about putting his baseball caps in the Outbox, he said they were non-negotiable. Many of them had been given to him by an old boss whom he admired greatly. Then I suggested that we put them on display, so that he could at least enjoy them.

"You're not putting them on display in our apartment!" Linda said, revealing another non-negotiable area.

"It's fine," Dan said. "Why don't we just put them back in the closet? Stack them up in the back or something. I don't need to see them; I just want to keep them."

Using a little ingenuity and the installation of a desperately needed light fixture inside Dan's closet, we managed to hang all of Dan's hats on the upper walls inside his closet, where they could be seen and wouldn't fall down. Dan, who had not originally cared for this part of the process, was ecstatic. "Now that's a nice hat collection!" he said proudly. Linda agreed and was particularly pleased that she never had to pick them up again.

Move All Old Mail, Catalogs, and Magazines to the Outbox. Sort through all your mail; move bills and personal correspondence into two neat piles. Everything else, including old mail, catalogs, and magazines, is to be put in the Outbox. It doesn't matter if you haven't read any of it. It isn't going anywhere. Carefully stack it so that you can decide what to do with it later. Right now you are clearing the decks.

Look into What You Would Need to Create a Landing Strip. Everyone should have a system for sorting the good stuff from all the useless material that the world constantly tries to push into our mailbox. To be most effective, sorting should take place at the door, while you still have the chance to manage it easily without having to think about it twice.

To do this, you need to imagine the front hall as a big filter for the outside world. Many companies make a living trying to get our attention and grab our eyeballs. You should value your time at home highly and not give your eyeballs away easily. Therefore, don't open junk mail. Don't keep magazines or catalogs you haven't ordered. With a good filter, many things may approach, but nothing gets into your home unless it is good for you.

A healthy filter at your front door should have three parts: a doormat, a coat hook, and a Landing Strip. The doormat keeps the dirt out. The coat hook or hangers provide a place to put your coat, bag, boots, shoes, umbrella, or dog leash. This keeps the city grime and water out of your living spaces. The Landing Strip is where you can lay things down and sort the mail along with your change, keys, and other odds and ends that come out of your pockets at the end of a long day.

Just as a plane requires a long runway for landing, your Landing Strip needs to have plenty of room and be kept clear. Your Landing Strip should anticipate the sorts of things that you bring home each day.

All mail can be loosely broken down into three categories: personal and social, bills and finance, and shopping and entertainment. Personal and social correspondence is the most important and usually the smallest category. These envelopes may rarely seem pressing, but they deserve your first response. This mail concerns your relationships with others and organizations that you might belong to. All of this should be read immediately, kept in a basket or box on your Landing Strip, and responded to within one week. Social announcements or calendars may be pinned to a bulletin board in the same location, and these should be rotated immediately as soon as a new one comes in.

Bills and financial correspondence constitute the second most important category. It concerns your financial relationship with the world and consists of bills, bank statements, mortgage statements, and loan notices, as well as any other paperwork that is used to administer your finances. Unless you don't know what it is or have fallen behind on your regular bill-paying schedule, this mail does not need to be read immediately and should be placed in a separate basket or box on your Landing Strip. It should be responded to monthly.

The last category is the biggest, the heaviest, and the most troublesome. It is also the least important. This consists of entertainment, information, and shopping or event opportunities that are coming to you solicited and unsolicited. This includes so-called junk mail. This category can grow very quickly, so it should be sorted daily, with those items that you would like to take time over placed in another basket or box on or near your Landing Strip. This should be cleared out every week. If you find that you have more than one issue of the same magazine piling up, it is time to throw one out and make more room.

Consider how these categories impact your life. If you threw out everything in the first category for a month, it would be an irreplaceable personal loss. If you did the same for the second category, you would receive a follow-up the next month and you might sustain a small financial loss. However, if you threw out everything in the third category for a month, you would lose nothing of personal or financial value. You would only be gaining time in your life and room in your apartment. So why is it so hard to reduce this third category?

Catalog, magazine, and direct-mail marketing companies do such an excellent job of creating glossy, attractive, and important-looking items that it usually feels wrong to throw them away. But you must for the simple reason that it does no good to take time over or respond to everything the world sends your way. Proactive people choose the things they want to spend their life doing and avoid the random demands of others.

Stephen Covey outlined an extremely helpful way of categorizing and breaking down the types of activities that take up our day in *The Seven Habits of Highly Effective People*. I have found it helpful to classify all of the mail that comes in your door in a similar way:

1. Important and urgent
   a. Overdue bills
   b. Overdue business or personal correspondence

2. Important and not urgent
   a. Personal letters
   b. Bills
   c. Official business correspondence
   d. Some magazines or periodicals
   e. Some event announcements

3. Not important and urgent
   a. Introductory offers
   b. Catalogs you have purchased from

    c.   Magazines you subscribe to
    d.   Event announcements

4. Not important and not urgent
    a.   All other advertisements, catalogs, magazines, and junk mail requesting your attention

They key to this categorization is realizing that you don't want to be constantly dealing with mail when it is in the first category. To prevent this, you want to nip things in the bud and deal with them when they are less urgent and still in the second category, "important and not urgent." Keep dealing with everything that comes in your door at this stage of the game and you will be happy.

Categories three and four should be diverted immediately. Put category four mail in the garbage and be *very careful* about category three. The number of magazines and catalogs you keep should include only those you actually look at each week.

Cancel Any Unused Subscriptions. One good way to keep categories three and four down to a minimum is to cancel subscriptions to all catalogs, magazines, and other mailing lists that you may be on. You will find that it can easily be done over the phone in less than half an hour, while the relief you will feel by not getting all that mail will last for months. Eventually, as you purchase things you will get on new lists and the mail will grow again, but doing this once or twice a year will keep this problem at bay.

Heart

Identify Cool Rooms and Warm Rooms. Flow between rooms is greatly enhanced through the use of different colors in each room. Cool colors (blues, greens, grays) are contracting and calming; warm colors (reds, yellows, oranges) are expansive and stimulating.

Just as breathing is made up of contraction (the in breath) and expansion (the out breath), you want to feel this movement as you walk through your apartment. This is done by alternating warm and cool colors.

Certain rooms lend themselves readily to one or the other, so it is good to use these as a starting point:

Area	Movement	Color
1. Hallway	Contraction	Cool
2. Kitchen	Expansion	Warm
3. Dining room	Expansion	Warm
4. Living room	Expansion	Warm
5. Office	Contraction	Cool
6. Bathroom	Contraction	Cool
7. Bedroom	Contraction	Cool

Whether you are working on one room or many, look closely at each room of your apartment and determine whether it is or could be considered a warm or cool room.

If you are working on a One-Room Remedy, you will be making color changes this week, while in the Deep Treatment, you should simply work to develop your awareness of color in your home and make any small adjustments that you wish. See the box on page 113 for a short course in color that will help you become more confident when choosing colors.

Apply the 80/20 Color Rule. Use strong colors sparingly. Allow them to punctuate a room, not define it.

In any room, I recommend 80 percent neutral and 20 percent strong colors. Just as a woman will make up her face by applying neutral colors to most areas and then highlight her lips and eyes, a room should be similarly balanced. For example, in Mike's living room, I suggested off-white walls (warm/neutral) to go with his rich brown couches (warm/neutral). Adding a deep red rug (warm/color) and table lamps in black, silver, or red (warm/color) would wake up the room. Small batches of color have a tremendous effect on the whole and will bring out the neutral colors around them.

Tamara's Studio

At our first meeting in her studio apartment, Tamara showed me magazine clippings of rooms she liked. I asked her if any of these photos gave her ideas for wall colors. She was unsure. On one hand, she wanted the apartment to be white, "so it would seem bigger," but on the other, she wanted it to be livelier, colorful, and a little funky. When I asked her what colors she liked, she held up one picture in particular. In it was a bright white room with a sage green couch, off-white carpet, brown bamboo bowl, and bright orange flowers sticking out of a vase. The colors reflected a warm, tropical influence. "Organic modern," I thought.

Inspired by her choice, I suggested that we use this group of colors in her room. She thought that meant painting the walls orange, brown, and green, and was not amused. I explained that we could use this photograph as a "color family." I suggested that we try to match the colors already in her apartment with those in the photograph.

COLOR 101

Mike bought two beautiful brown modern couches and then a soft blue rug to go in front of them. But something still wasn't right in his living room. Laura wanted to paint her bedroom green, ended up trying three different shades, and still was not happy. Sarah wanted to be safe, so she went with a lot of neutral colors in her apartment. Then she wished it all had more color, but she didn't feel comfortable deciding where to put those touches.

Color is powerful. It can be stimulating, healing, soothing, and fun. Getting color right can be tricky, and choosing can signal a big commitment. Given the amount of money that most people spend decorating their living room, the thought of buying an armchair in a colorful fabric can be downright terrifying. If it doesn't work, you are stuck with it. That is why most people play it safe by buying things in neutral colors like beige and brown.

In order to make good choices with color, you need to know how to differentiate between warm and cool colors, as well as how to find a color family.

Warm Colors and Cool Colors
The color palette is divided between warm colors and cool colors. Reds, yellows, oranges, beige, and creamy colors are warm. Blues, greens, and grays are cool. If you look at the color wheel, which you may remember from elementary school, the warm colors are on one side of the wheel and the cool colors on

the other. Where they overlap, they form mixtures such as green (blue + yellow) and purple (blue + red). These hybrids can be warmer or cooler depending on their mix. For example, lime green has a lot of yellow in it, so it is warm, whereas kelly green has more blue in it, so it is cool.

Warm Colors Are Stimulating

Red, orange, and yellow are fire colors; they are hot and stimulating. Even off-whites with hints of these colors can have this effect. Whether we love or hate these colors, they are more emotionally reactive. This is the reason red is the most successful color for advertising and favored in such iconic places as the Coca-Cola label, Ferrari cars, and a woman's choice of bright red lipstick.

Because of their stimulating nature, warm colors are social and are often found in restaurants and bars. In our homes they serve us best in the social rooms of the house, such as the living room, dining room, and kitchen.

Cool Colors Are Calming

Green, blue, and purple calm our emotions and focus our thoughts. If our heart craves warmth, our head craves coolness. While it may be good to be hot-blooded when in love, it is definitely not to our advantage to be hotheaded when working on a mathematical equation. This is why the cool blues are the most popular color for business suits and police uniforms, why the old-time bank teller wore a green visor, and why the Yankees are considered gentlemen in their blue pinstripes (while the Red Sox have long been considered fiery warriors).

Because of their calming nature, cool colors are supportive of our mental life and can be found in schools, offices, and hospitals. In our homes, they serve us best in the quieter rooms of the house, such as the bedroom, office, and nursery.

A Short Note on Black and White

Though black and white are not considered colors (white is the absence of color, black the combination of all colors), they do have warm and cool properties: white is cool and black is warm. When you paint a room straight white, it will be cool. Therefore, white rooms require some warm color or other warm element for balance in order to make them physically comfortable. Black adds warmth, but its darkness can easily overwhelm a room, and so it should be used sparingly.

A Short Note on Neutral Colors

Neutral colors are the mutts of the color world: they are easygoing, fit in most places, and don't offend, but they lack a strong defining character. Neutrals cover a dizzyingly vast landscape of color that runs from the warm red-brown of milk chocolate to the cooler taupes and stone colors and the light beige off-whites. While rarely thrilling in their own right, they become more exciting and sophisticated in a group with a stronger color in their midst.

Be Consistent When Using Color!
With all this in mind, when you design a room, you need to decide in advance what kind of an effect you want in the room, whether it is going to be predominantly warm or cool. Don't paint your kitchen green (cool) when you have a terra-cotta floor (warm) and gold-finish hardware (warm). Don't put down a blue carpet (cool) in your living room if you have brown couches and off-white walls (warm). Don't mix warm and cool palettes unless you want your room to be purposely funky or offbeat.

The green in the photo was close to that of her couch. The natural brown of the bamboo bowl was close to the natural brown of her floor. What we had left to work in was the off-white and the bright orange. "Where will we put the bright orange?" she asked skeptically. I suggested the wall at the entrance to the room. She thought it would be too much.

I pressed her to consider it, since she wanted her apartment to be more colorful and funky. By painting one wall and partially obscuring it with bookshelves, her studio would come to life but not be overwhelmed by the new color. When Tamara decided to go for it, she was consoled by the fact that she could paint it over if she didn't like it.

She didn't need to. The color warmed her entire apartment and defined it for her friends. We were filmed doing this project for the television show Mission: Organization, and I still get calls and e-mails from people who loved the apartment and remember the orange wall. I remind everyone who asks that this was Tamara's color, not a decorator's idea. She found the color family; I just urged her to trust her instincts and follow through with it.

Color Families

When choosing colors it is helpful to know which ones go together. A color family is a set of colors that work well together. For example, on the Fourth of July, primary red, white, and blue make a complete color family; anything you decorate with these three colors will fit in. Imagine that you decided to change the blue slightly to a pale light blue. The modified group of primary red, white, and pale blue wouldn't feel quite right. You would have interrupted the familiar (patriotic) color family. If you changed the blue to primary green, you would all of a sudden have a different country's celebration. Colors are powerful, and color families tend to be exclusive in what they signify and how they make us feel.

The easiest way to find a color family is to look at nature. For example, fall has a red and brown color family, while spring gets its colors from fresh green shoots of grass and the bright hues of the season's first flowers. Color families can draw from the colors of a whole season, or from just one object in nature: a tulip, moss on a rock, or a shell on the beach. Color families also shift as you move around the world. For example, India has a far different set of color families from New England.

When Martha Stewart and her colleagues were creating a new line of paints, they chose as their inspiration the colors found in the shells of Auracana hen eggs—soft blues, off-whites, greens, and grays. They created a collection of paints based entirely on this color family, called the Auracana Collection.

Because this collection was a true color family, coming directly from nature, all of the colors could be used together in any combination and remain in harmony. In fact, I used this collection throughout an entire house, and the result was a home whose rooms felt perfectly in tune with one another. By using one color family, you can safely choose *any* of its colors and get great results.

If you don't have time to drive through New England noting the fall colors or closely studying the eggshells of a particular type of bird, another way of finding a color family is by looking closely at rooms and objects designers have already made. Catalogs and shelter magazines will have photographs of rooms based on color families, like the tropical motif Tamara showed to me. Single objects can also inspire your color family, such as a favorite Persian rug, a blanket, or a painting.

Head

Cook Two Meals at Home This Week. Continue the cooking you started last week, and expand it to two nights a week. If you want to be adventurous, find a new recipe. Use your kitchen, keep a fresh flow of food moving into and out of your refrigerator, and don't forget to do your dishes each night.

This last point is an important one. If you are in the habit of leaving dishes in the sink overnight, now is the time to stop. Be sure that you wash all dishes by the end of every day and leave the sink and all counters clear and wiped down. We want to promote better flow in this area, so it makes no sense to create new clutter if you are using it more. Additionally, since all clutter is really the result of delayed decision making, don't delay your decisions in the kitchen. Get in the habit of not only washing dishes when you are done with them, but also throwing food out as soon as you notice it going bad, and restocking any item as soon as you notice that it is running low.

Design an Invitation for Your Housewarming. This is a fun, creative activity. It may feel years away, but if you want people to reserve the date to come to your housewarming, the earlier you get the invitation out the better.

Whether you choose to invite friends by letter or via e-mail, take a little time this week to choose the words and/or a design for your invitations and send them off. I have had clients buy elaborate stationery and write florid invitations with a fountain pen, while others have put together a colorful graphic on their computers and used **Evite.** I recommend the former; the more personal it is, the better, but a simple handwritten note will do. Use this opportunity to express your style and alert your guests to the fact that you are inviting them to a housewarming after your Eight-Week Cure is finished. If they have never heard of an apartment Cure and they know your apartment well, it will be sure to catch their attention.

One-Room Remedy

Research Your Shopping List. This week you should begin to look for the items on your Shopping List in the style and price range you have settled on. A tremendous amount of this research can be done online, as most major stores and many smaller ones have Web sites where they display their inventory. The Stores Guide at www.apartmenttherapy.com will provide you with a good list of stores in different styles, most of which offer shipping. I recommend starting online and then following up by visiting actual stores whenever possible.

Start a List of Proposed Interior Changes. If you haven't already, it is time to start your Interior Design Worksheet.

By now, you probably have a number of ideas of things you would like to do, and you should be collecting them all in one place. Take time to jot down the changes you have thought about for your room. You can make a copy of this sheet in the Appendix or at apartmenttherapy.com, in order to work more freely.

Identify Cool Rooms and Warm Rooms. Continuing with the work you did in Week Two, you will identify whether you are working on a cool or warm room. If the room is currently a mixture of warm and cool, decide which it should be. Use your Interior Design Worksheet to record which elements might be removed and/or what steps would be required to focus this room.

Determine Whether Window Treatments Are Necessary. Many clients have reservations about window treatments and don't have them when we begin our work together. A typical reason for avoiding window treatments is to let in as much light as possible. "I don't want to cover my windows," clients have said. "I want the light. It will be too dark if I cover them." Sometimes they don't say it, but I can tell they are thinking, "He is telling me I need curtains. That is so typical. That is such a decorator's solution, to cover everything up and add frilly fabric everywhere. Doesn't he know I like my windows the way they are?" Or "He just doesn't get it. I like to see my windows and the frames. They are cool modern details. Curtains are so traditional."

I have stood in tense face-offs with clients more times over this issue than over any other. Nell and Jack had a beautiful loft on the top floor of a building in SoHo. Two entire sides of their apartment had eight-foot-tall windows running the length of the walls. As you came in the door those windows made a stunning vista. The couple had me over to help them plan for the arrival of their first child, who was due in one month. Everything was going fine until I mentioned curtaining the hall windows so that light wouldn't flood the nursery. Nell liked the idea, but all of a sudden it was clear that Jack was extremely uncomfortable with the way the conversation was going.

They had a beautiful, expensive loft space with tremendous industrial architectural details, including these huge windows. The whole aesthetic was open, sunny, and clean—very modern. The thought of a traditional curtain set him off. This was not surprising. Most city dwellers with a modern sensibility have a deep resistance to curtains specifically and window treatments in general, but they are missing out on a very beautiful and practical part of interior design.

First, curtains are powerful accents that highlight the natural beauty of windows. They should rarely cover the window, but rather sit at the side with their tall linear shape drawing one's eye to the height of the window, making it seem bigger. Modern curtains aren't pulled to the side in a traditional way, but hang straight down without pleats or traditional patterns. They also should not be opaque, but have a translucent quality that allows light through, creating a more sophisticated interplay of light within each room.

Second, curtains are a superior design for controlling the flow of light through windows. They are easy to install, easy to move, and easy to clean. The same cannot be said for shades or blinds. All of these, however, are necessary for filtering the strong energy flows coming from outside that otherwise will overstimulate your home and fade your furniture.

Windows without any type of covering may be dramatic

and attractive, but in my opinion they are the equivalent of having eyes without eyelids. Your windows are the eyes of your home, and they should have a protective membrane around them that can open and close as needed.

Apply the 80/20 Color Rule. At this point you have decided which of your rooms are warm and which are cool, and you are familiar with the 80/20 rule that will add emotional energy to your apartment (see 80/20 rule in this week's Deep Treatment section). Now is the time for your color assessment.

For Those Who Don't Have Enough Color

Most people have too little color in their homes. Look around your room. Do strong colors pop out at you? Do you see a great expanse of beige, white, and middle-of-the-road muddy browns? Is any piece of furniture playing a starring color role, or are you surrounded by a well-trained chorus of B-list performers? If you sense that your apartment could use some more color, consider adding it in the following accessories: pillows (on sofa), lamp shades, rugs, lamp bases, throw blankets, curtains, a vase with flowers, a picture or painting, or paint on one wall. You may add any number of these listed elements in either a warm or cool color, but do not let it exceed more than 20 percent of the overall room. Enter your choices on your Interior Design Worksheet.

Matthew had a great living room, but it was all brown and beige. To spice it up he added a red rug, two bright pillows for his couch, and a sharp, colorful photograph of Cuba that he found through a friend. Peter, a real estate agent, dressed up an apartment he was selling by simply adding fresh flowers to the dining table, a bowl full of red apples to the coffee table and a colorful throw blanket across the couch. Michael and Laurie added a sage green rug in their living room along with two shiny mercury glass lamps, and painted the walls a warm peachy color. Susan's bathroom walls changed from white to a sea green, which now stood out more against the white tiles. In all of these cases, the rooms only began to show some emotion and attract attention with these infusions of color.

For Those Who Have Too Much Color

Some people have too much color in their apartment, or they have opposing warm and cool colors that are causing some heart-level discord. People who have this problem often have a hard time with color in general. While you can't change your ability to detect colors, with help you can be sure that you are collecting either warm or cool colors in each room.

Assessing your room, with help if needed, you should decide what needs to be removed so that it is either warm or cool and consists of only 20 percent strong or bright colors. If you have large pieces of furniture with strong colors, you can remove the smaller objects found in the list above, and if you have many small colorful objects, simply edit them back by depositing the extras in your Outbox or moving them to other rooms (if that helps the other rooms). If you want to keep an object in the room but it has too much color on it, consider re-covering or slipcovering it.

At the end of this week, you should have added to your Interior Design Worksheet a group of colorful items, removed certain items from each room, or noted that you wish to re-cover or replace certain elements with less color.

Research and Call In Help This Week. If you haven't started on this already, now is the time to research and call in help. Don't be shy! Knowing when and how to get help is a higher art. While doing it yourself is a virtue, don't confuse this with doing *everything* yourself. Many hands make light work, and your job is to manage this project, not necessarily to carry every armchair up every staircase.

Hiring someone else to paint for you is highly recommended if you have given yourself very ambitious goals for these eight weeks. While I find painting extremely relaxing and an excellent way to get to know your apartment intimately, it does take time if you are an amateur. Professional painters will be much faster and are one of the more affordable services you can hire.

While it is important to know how something works, if you trust people and choose wisely, having others share their gifts with you not only creates a better result, but also enriches your life via the relationship that forms, no matter how temporary. The best people you hire will be the ones who teach you something new. My accountant, Andrew, is a genius, and I love going to see him once a year. He has given me insights into the subject of taxes that I don't think I ever would have had by myself.

Word of Mouth

Word of mouth is the best way to find help. And one of the great advantages to apartment living is that there are many people near you, who live in apartments similar to yours, who have done some kind of work in them. Therefore, the best place to find help or a reference is right inside your own building.

If speaking to your doorman, super, or neighbors doesn't reveal the person you need to paint, hang curtains, or install a bathroom floor, here are good places to go for references: www.apartmenttherapy.com in New York and Los Angeles, local hardware stores and lumberyards, and local real estate brokers.

Most plumbing, tile, and kitchen stores provide their own servicepeople or have a list that they will recommend, so if nothing else works, using your yellow pages and calling this type of store directly will often yield results.

The goal here is to find two or three references for the work you are considering. You then want to call and meet these people in your apartment, sharing with them your clear list of jobs that they can help you with. Be honest, be detailed, and then see how they respond. This is what you want to learn from them:

1. If they can handle the job
2. How they would go about it
3. When they can do it
4. How much they estimate it would cost
5. What they expect from you in the way of help

Obviously, for bigger jobs there is going to be more pressure and a longer conversation, but even if it's a small job, being as clear as possible from the beginning will ensure a smooth working relationship.

Choosing the right person is a matter of intuition as well as numbers, and you want to make sure you can get along and communicate clearly with the person you choose. Here are other things to look for:

1. Don't go with the lowest bid. (This is an old saw, but it works.)
2. Choose a realist who can see and discuss problems ahead of time.
3. Look for a problem solver.

4. Go for the person who wants to do this work, not the one who is doing you a favor.
5. Look for someone who will be on your job, not running around to others.
6. Pick someone who is on time to meet you.
7. Go for the individual who isn't in a rush to leave.

For big jobs, choosing the right person is especially important because every big job comes with its own can of worms. On big jobs, you will inevitably discover something surprising and difficult in the process that will cause stress and throw you off balance. This is unavoidable. You cannot possibly anticipate all of the things that will come up in a kitchen renovation, and you will be forced to deal with some crises on the fly, causing changes to your budget and the timing of the job. When this happens, you want someone you can talk to and work with to solve problems.

In my experience, I have found that most service providers want to do a good job, and few of them are getting rich doing it. Sure, they want to make money, but the best way for them to make money is not to gouge you but to finish your job, get a good reference, and move on to the next customer. Therefore the most common tension occurs when the job begins to get extended but the client wants the budget to stay the same. The solution here is either to pay more for their time or to figure out how to get the job done with less work. This can be a difficult conversation, which is why you need to do your very best to find someone you can work with.

Susan's Dating Game

Susan had interviewed three contractors about redoing her one-bedroom apartment. Afterward, we met and she expressed confusion about what she should do next.

"The problem is," she said, "I liked Phil the best, but he is the most expensive, and I liked Gerald the least, but he came in with the lowest numbers. Anthony I liked, but he is in the middle."

Susan was redoing her whole kitchen, installing built-in shelving in her living room, rewiring the entire apartment, and painting. Her estimates looked like this:

Gerald	$25,000-$30,000
Anthony	$28,000
Phil	$33,000-$40,000

"Whom do you want to work with?" I asked her.

"Phil, but I can't afford forty thousand dollars."

"Then tell him that. Be honest with him. His estimate is a first pass. Go back to him and tell him you want to work with him. Tell him your budget, thirty thousand dollars, and see if by working together and sharpening your pencils, you can figure it out. He may lower some of his prices and you may take some things out of the basket. Either you will discover that it is possible or he will step away from taking the job, which is fine at this point. Then you can approach Anthony."

"Gosh, this is just like dating," Susan said without missing a beat.

"You're right. And at this point it is better to be

up-front and walk away if necessary than to have a bad breakup a few weeks down the line."

While humorous, once the dating metaphor became clear, Susan had no trouble figuring out how to choose a contractor.

Chapter Seven

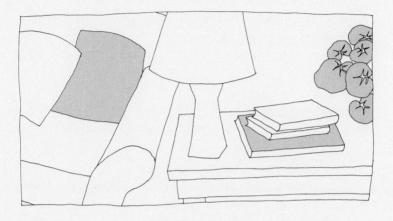

Week Four:
Retail Therapy

Nancy's green-striped room was gone, painted a beautiful bone white, but it was now totally empty and waiting for furniture. Finding it was slow going.

"We could do wall-mounted shelving or built-ins," I said. "I wouldn't recommend buying bookshelves for this room, as they won't tie into the wall and will make the room feel smaller."

"But the wall-mounted shelving you showed me looks

too cheap. It really doesn't look substantial enough, and the idea of built-ins just seems bulky. Isn't there anything else you can recommend?"

I couldn't. I had to admit that I had given Nancy my best ideas and was confused by her vacillation between pinching pennies and not liking the more affordable options. I gave up on the shelving and worked on other things. A few weeks went by, and then I received a call from Nancy in a state of excitement.

"I've found it! But I want you to see it today and tell me what you think."

"What?" I said. "Where are you?"

"I'm in the store and it's perfect shelving! It's called Vitsoe. It's a little expensive, but I love it. It's at this store in SoHo. Can you see it today?"

Incomparable in her ability to sniff out things she loved, Nancy had discovered a great resource and one that would become a favorite of mine as well.

Vitsoe shelving is a very light, modern metal shelving system with beautiful, clean lines and a distinctive support column that attaches to both floor and ceiling. It was designed by Dieter Rams in Germany in 1960 and has been in constant production ever since.

"I want to do the study and my bedroom in this stuff," she said excitedly.

Despite Vitsoe's beauty and classic design, the price for everything that Nancy wanted to do turned out to be too high, and she decided only to do her study. Even then, it stretched her budget, but she was willing to take a few things off her Shopping List to make up the difference.

When the shelving finally arrived and was installed, Nancy was delighted. It carried all of her books and became a focal point in the room, which lacked for other furniture because we hadn't found anything she liked yet.

"Nancy," I reminded her, "we have to finish this room."

"I know," she said, "but I don't want to spend my money on anything I don't like. I will keep looking."

I kept pushing, and slowly we made progress. Despite my frustration, I credited Nancy not only for having a great eye, but also for being stubborn enough not to make a decision she didn't believe in.

With only the shelving, a sofa, and a temporary desk, the room made Nancy very happy. "I love the room. It's beautiful," she would say every time I came over. And she was right.

Week Four: Deep Treatment

Bones
Clean up living room and related closets.
Repairs are being taken care of this week.

Breath
Declutter books and all media.
Cancel 75 percent of the catalogs you receive.
Empty Outbox this week.

Heart
Confirm what you need to increase or decrease color in each room.
Identify what you need to increase or decrease softness in each room.

Head
Cook three meals at home this week.
Send out your invitations.

Week Four: One-Room Remedy

Begin Shopping List and enter all prices into a spread-
sheet.
Decide on the total scope of work to be done.
Consider hiring a professional organizer.
Visit a paint store this week to find samples.

Deep Treatment

Bones

Clean Up Living Room and Related Closets. As you declutter your living room this week, make sure that you
get under everything and clean all surfaces, nooks, and
crannies. This is good for the bones. Many people never
move the big things in their apartments, like the books,
files, or television, and dust and grime builds up under
and behind all of these things.

Move everything so that you can wipe every surface,
including rugs, floor lamps, couches, chairs—anything
that sits on the floor or against a wall. As you do this, sort
through your possessions, add to the Outbox, and make
notes as to what you may need. Bookshelves that are
painted with latex paint age particularly badly, as books
have a tendency to stick to the paint and either cause a
mark, a stain, or both. Clean these well. As a tip for the
future, always use semigloss paint on bookshelves (semigloss enamel if your building will allow it—enamel,
which can now be found with a water base, is much
harder and much more durable under books and other
objects).

WOOD FLOORS

Even floors that have been hidden under objects, furniture, or carpeting will endure ordinary wear and tear. Once you have cleared space, you may notice that your floor is ready to be refinished or that a carpet needs replacement. Make a note of it! Many apartments have wood parquet on the floor, which is not refinished very often, either by owners or landlords. One client, who had hired me to help her furnish her apartment, no longer noticed that the part of her apartment most in need of help was the sad wood floor. The sealant had worn off, leaving the bare wood to turn patchy and gray. Instead of telling her to put her money into her furniture, I urged her to invest first in refinishing her floor.

While refinishing a wood floor is a disruptive procedure, it isn't as expensive as people generally think: it costs about the same as painting the walls and it can be done very quickly. Only a few years ago, it used to take twenty-four hours for one coat of polyurethane to dry, and most floors required at least three coats, but there are newer water-based polyurethanes that will dry in six hours, allowing you to lay down two coats a day. These are also a lot less toxic.

If you look at your floors and see that the wood is exposed and looks gray or dirty, consider refinishing them, and don't put it off until later.

Repairs Are Being Taken Care of This Week. This is ongoing. If you aren't saving repairs for a carpenter or contractor who will be working in your apartment soon, be sure that repairs on your Repair Worksheet are being taken care of this week. After this week, you have only two more weeks remaining in which to get these done.

Breath

Declutter Books and All Media. In the living room you are going to get into the thick of things. This is generally where most items such as books, photographs, and papers are kept. This week, weed out all the clutter and extra belongings you have accumulated and send them right to the Outbox.

Books

Declutter your book collection this week. Books should not fill the shelves to bursting; a good rule of thumb is to leave at least 10 percent as open space. Books should sit neatly upright on the shelf, positioned about one inch back from the front of the shelf. Many people try to maximize shelf space by storing books behind books. This never looks good, and you'll never find what you are looking for. It is better to keep everything in sight and organized. Here is a typical shelf system: fiction (alphabetical by author) includes sections for novels, poetry, and plays; nonfiction (alphabetical by title) includes sections for biographies, business and finance, children's, history, and self-help.

If you choose to store your books flat for any reason, do it neatly! Put larger books on the bottom and smaller ones on top, and keep their front edges straight.

Put as many books in the Outbox as you can. Books are good resources and markers of experience, but we all tend to hold on to far more than we actually use. To ease the process, it is helpful to realize that books are collections of memories and old thoughts, not new ones; they carry an emotional weight as well as a physical one. On this subject, I have often quoted Karen Kingston's words from *Creating Sacred Space with Feng Shui* to my clients: "Holding on to old books doesn't allow you to create space for new ideas and ways of thinking to come into your life."

Not only is letting go clearing out the old, it is also trusting in the future. If you have never gotten rid of any books, aim to reduce your collection by at least 25 percent this week.

CDs, DVDs, and Videos

Nowadays, CDs, DVDs, and videos are almost as hard for people to part with as books. This is a shame, since the physical material of these is inferior to books and so incompatible with a healthy home. They are also far less attractive to look at.

For music CDs, I heartily recommend transferring all music to a computer hard drive and either storing, selling, or giving away your CDs. While computers have created many new stresses in our modern society, they have been extremely successful in allowing us to store and play music. Apple's products for computer music are terrific: **iTunes,** a digital jukebox, is an easy, free way to organize your music on a Mac or a PC, while Apple **Air-Ports** works very well for streaming music from your computer to anywhere in your house. Portable digital musical devices such as **iPods** make it easy to transport your music with you and keep multiple copies for backup.

Many people that I know have made the switch from playing CDs to playing files off their computer. Clients to whom I have introduced it catch on very quickly and never go back. While some people miss the jacket art, iTunes and other players are already integrating jacket art features as well.

One friend, Bea, took all of her CDs to her office in shopping bags and over a two-week period imported them all into her computer before transferring them to her iPod. Afterward, she took the bags of CDs to a store in her neighborhood and sold them all for $100. She was at first shocked that she got only a small fraction of what she had paid for them, but when I reminded her that she still had the music, and now she also had $100 in cash, she saw that it was a remarkably better deal.

Videos

We don't copy movies and walk around with them as we now do with music, so I find movies are best treated as one treats books: keep a few of the ones that are really dear to you or hard to find, and let the others go into the Outbox.

Cancel 75 Percent of the Catalogs You Receive. Catalogs are like heat-seeking missiles: they find where we live and they never stop coming. At one point, I was receiving so many catalogs that my mailman could not put my mail in my box and would have to leave it by my door. When my future wife and I moved in together after we became engaged, she took one look at my mail situation and said it had to stop. She stacked up every one of the catalogs we had received that month and called each of the toll-free customer service numbers. The calls went very quickly, and miraculously all the catalogs soon stopped arriving. The pounds of mail that I was used to receiving returned to a small pile of letters, and I couldn't have been happier.

When I was a child, I used to look forward to coming home after school and reading a new catalog, glossy and attractive, with a glass of milk and cookies. Getting a new catalog was almost like having a product from the store itself. When I went to other people's houses, I would notice their catalogs and find myself judging who they were by which ones they received.

Catalogs signify what we could buy, what we like, and what our style is. Even if we are not ordering from them, receiving them reinforces our own style, and the fact that they "want" us still feels good. In our consumer-based culture, just being near the heat of a possible purchase warms the soul.

In light of this, canceling catalog subscriptions can feel like a lonely-making, possibly suicidal act. It is nearly as threatening as turning off the television. Yet the reward truly outweighs the loss.

Empty Outbox This Week. There are many places that will happily take most every belonging in your Outbox and put it to good use. Here are a few options to think about:

1.   Find out what day or night the sanitation department picks up bulk items, put valuable items out on the

street prior to this time, and they'll be gone before the truck arrives.

2. Give to charity.

   a. Clothing and wood furniture (not particleboard) can be donated to charities such as Goodwill, the Salvation Army, Housing Works (in NYC), or houses of worship.
   b. Books are welcome at Housing Works, Goodwill, and your public library.

3. Give to friends. Inviting friends over to take things from your Outbox is one of the most satisfying ways of letting go. Some people organize "tag sale" cocktail parties and invite friends over to buy or take home their belongings.

4. If you want to make a few bucks, large and small items can easily be sold on www.craigslist.com, furniture can be sold at www.apartmenttherapy.com in NYC and LA, CDs are easily sold to local music shops, most used-book stores will buy hardcovers and give good money for art books, and yard or block sales are profitable and fun.

5. In addition, more and more items can be easily recycled: computers and electronic equipment recyclers can be found through www.wasteless.org; all household items can be recycled locally through www.freecycle.org, a Yahoo group that connects people who wish to give and receive without commercial interest; and all the rest—paper, glass, plastic, and metal—can now be recycled in most major cities.

Kate's Yearly Sale

Kate lived in San Francisco and had a tremendous clothes collection, which she was always adding to. Since she didn't have enough room or enough money to buy all of the clothes she wanted, she would stage a clothing sale in her home one weekend each year, tagging and selling off about 50 percent of her collection. Due to her good taste (and common dress size), her clothing sale became not only popular among her friends, but also very profitable and effective in emptying out her closets.

Kate's sale proved that you can get the most from your belongings if you manage a sale by yourself, and it is far more gratifying to deal with friends. Each year, after the sale, Kate had enough money to buy more clothes, and she had the added pleasure of being thanked every time she saw one of her friends wearing something from the sale.

Heart

Confirm What You Need to Increase or Decrease Color in Each Room. You started thinking last week about what bright or strong colors you could add or subtract from each room, and now is the time to finalize your choices. Remember that a little color goes a long way, and what you are looking for here is a homeopathic dose of color that will enliven your room, not a big makeover. When you are happy with your choices, put the items down on your Shopping List and take care of them this week.

Identify What You Need to Increase or Decrease Softness in Each Room. Softness or hardness is unlike color in that it wants to be balanced in a 50/50 way. Every apartment starts out as a hard shell, made up almost entirely of the mineral elements of stone, steel, and glass. In the course of making a home out of our space we bring in organic softness in the form of upholstery, rugs, curtains, blankets, pillows, and even plants.

Since we live in a world where the Modern style has overtaken all other styles, there is a tendency toward hard, mineral interiors and many people don't "pad" their nest enough. This leads to underlying discomfort, coldness, and poor acoustics. If you don't have any rugs or carpets on your floors or any curtains on your windows, you are probably in need of softness. Another way of checking your softness level is to clap your hands. If you can hear a faint echo or any reverberation off your walls, sounds are not being damped and your room needs softening. The materials of choice here are usually cotton, linen, or wool (it is best to avoid polyester or acrylic fibers, which are mineral-based, unless it helps with allergies or other health problems).

On the other hand, if you have many rugs and curtains in addition to clutter, tight spaces, and/or tons of books, you are probably in need of some firming up. Clearing off surfaces and paring back books and curtains will quickly free a room from being smothered in too much softness.

Look around your apartment. See if you can determine whether your home is evenly balanced between hard and soft. See what you could add or remove to balance your apartment.

Head

Cook three meals at home this week. As you expand your repertoire in the kitchen and freshen your food stock, try some new things in the kitchen this week.

The best way to kick-start creativity in the kitchen is to attempt to copy a meal you have just had at a restaurant or friend's house, and the second best way is to start from a recipe. While many recipes and recipe books assume a certain amount of experience, here are a number of good resources for simple, creative cooking:

1. *Newspapers:* "The Minimalist" by Mark Bittman in the *New York Times* Dining section each week has recipes, or check your own newspaper's style section.

2. *Online:* Recipes are available at Apartment Therapy: The Kitchen (apartmenttherapy.com). Also try www. epicurious.com, www.foodandwine.com, and www.foodtv. com.

3. *Books:* Among my favorites are the following classics, *Cucina Fresca: Italian Food, Simply Prepared* by Viana La Place, *The Zuni Cookbook* by Judy Rogers, *The Silver Palate Cookbook* by Julee Rosso and Sheila Lukins, and *The Chez Panisse Menu Cookbook* by Alice Waters.

Send Out Your Invitations. I know people who are very good at writing letters and very bad at sending them. Don't let this be you. Buy stamps and put your invitations in the mail by Sunday.

One-Room Remedy

Begin Shopping List and Enter All Prices into a Spreadsheet. It is challenging to take your vision as you have expressed it in your Style Tray and your floor plan and translate it into items that you can find in stores. A great deal of an interior designer's job is knowing where to find things and what is available. These sources are often jealously guarded trade secrets. Nowadays, however, you have tremendous retail resources available, and many high-end vendors will sell directly to retail clients.

As you navigate the world of purchasing, it helps to understand how the market is structured. Here is a rough sketch of what you will find:

Typical retail:

Items are manufactured in large quantities.
Division consists of large companies and chains.
Everybody pays the same, unless you buy in bulk.

Better retail:

Items are manufactured in small quantities.
Division consists of medium-sized companies and designer stores.
Retail customers pay full price.
Designers get small discount: 10–30 percent off.

High-end/custom-made:

Items are handmade to order.
Division consists of small companies and individual craftspeople.
Retail customers pay full price.
Designers get large discount: 25–50 percent off.

In my work with clients, I have shopped mainly within the first two categories and been very happy with the results. In the world of typical retail, good design, international manufacturing, and a massive interest in improving the home have all conspired to produce numerous affordable resources. With creativity and resourcefulness one can find many of the basic building blocks for furnishing your home from stores like IKEA, Crate & Barrel, Williams-Sonoma, and Pottery Barn. I use these resources with high-end and budget clients alike, as do many other interior designers. There are a few tricks to doing this well, however:

1. If the price seems too low, watch out! You usually get what you pay for.
2. Don't buy everything from one store.
3. Keep your intake of cheaper chipboard and veneer furniture to a minimum (not more than 30 percent).
4. Kick the tires—make sure an item is well made before you buy it.
5. Look for furniture staples in these stores and go elsewhere for decorative pieces.

On a number of occasions I have considered building a table or shelf for a client only to be stopped by the walloping high price. One of my high-end resources, Ronald Signorelli, who builds custom-made desks and cabinets that can cost up to $50,000 apiece, once told me, "Don't build it yourself unless you have a lot of money. Go look at Crate & Barrel. They do a good job and no one can compete with their prices."

When I asked him how come their prices were so much lower, he said, "Because they make their furniture in quantity. If you make things in quantity, you can really bring down the price. Anytime you build something once, such as in a custom situation, you have to pay for the full cost of making it."

It is true. While we have all grown used to the furniture prices we see commonly advertised at national stores such as IKEA, where a sofa can cost $300, we have forgotten that these prices do not reflect the real cost of building an individual piece of furniture. These prices can only be achieved by very large companies that can manage to produce and sell furniture in quantity.

Smaller stores and manufacturers who pay a living wage to skilled craftspeople in this country have to charge a lot more for a sofa. In most cases, there is a huge difference in the quality, and you are buying something that will last far longer and be a better investment. This is not a pitch for spending a lot of money; rather, spend it conscientiously. Don't always think you are getting a great deal when something costs less than you expect, and don't always think you are getting cheated when something costs more than you expect. All of these resources have something to offer, and the smartest shoppers pick and choose.

Jemma and Kevin Don't Shop, They Collect

Working with Jemma and Kevin was a revelation. They lived in a small one-bedroom apartment and needed help with rearranging and organization. Jemma and Kevin rarely shopped for furniture. Instead they had inherited most of their furniture from his parents and had made a few purchases over the years of some very nice pieces. They had a small Ralph Lauren love seat in leather that Kevin commented on: "I usually hate Ralph Lauren, and it was really expensive, but it was perfect for our apartment and I really wanted it."

They had a dining room table that Jemma's cousin had made for them as a wedding present. It was a simple Shaker design, about six feet long, and it fit quietly into the room. There was a lot of art. Kevin liked to collect photographs and pictures done by friends and acquaintances. They had only one printed poster on their walls: a large vintage art print of a French liqueur, which Kevin had purchased nearly ten years earlier.

To light up the room, however, they had found small halogen spotlights at IKEA, which brightly illuminated two small carved stone horses. To organize their papers, they had found a terrific wood rolling file from Hold Everything. Amidst the antiques and interesting furniture that they had collected, there were many subtle infusions of products from the lower-priced chain stores. I would say that in their apartment they had 80 percent antique, handmade, and expensive furniture and 20 percent totally inexpensive off-the-shelf accessories or furniture.

In the course of rearranging and reorganizing their apartment, I came to see the genius of this in terms of furnishing the home. Kevin had been collecting nice furniture a little at a time since graduating from college. Almost everything he and Jemma had bought still lived in their apartment and wasn't dingy, falling apart from use, or long out of fashion. This stuff was built to last, and it made their home feel distinctly personal, comfortable, and stylish. It also made their apartment more vibrant.

Jemma and Kevin had never gone and bought a bedroom set or a sectional sofa with two matching chairs and a coffee table all at once. Instead they bought a bed and at another time they bought a nightstand. If they needed other things and couldn't afford them, they waited. They were not afraid of empty space, and after a few years even that wasn't a problem. Eventually, just like everyone else, they had too many things and needed to sell or give something away.

Atkins for Furniture: Protein vs. Carbohydrates

I have found that when most people shop for furniture they look at price and try to buy the most furniture they can for the money they can spend. But not all furniture is created equal, and it is very important that you know this before you spend any money. I recommend to clients that they approach shopping from various sources differently and think about what they are doing.

Most people:

1. Spread their money out
2. Have many inexpensive pieces and only a few nice pieces
3. Have too much furniture
4. End up having to throw out or replace furniture every five years

In light of this, it is preferable to:

1. Concentrate your money and buy good furniture
2. Have more quality pieces and fewer inexpensive ones

It was while I was working at Jemma and Kevin's that I began to see furniture differently. I began to see that among that broad category of home furnishings and accessories, what we purchase falls into one of two categories: protein or carbohydrate. Like the food groups these labels represent, the former provides much more long-lasting service than the latter. Because my approach reminds me of the emphasis placed upon protein in the Atkins Diet, I refer to this as an "Atkins furniture diet."

Most homes are filled with carbohydrate furniture. This is the relatively stylish, inexpensive furniture that is made of pressboard, plywood, and veneer with faux finishes to mimic solid wood. While I love the Swedish giant IKEA dearly, this is primarily what the chain sells. There is nothing wrong with this furniture except that the quality of its manufacture and the simplicity of its style are indications that its life will be short. Furniture like this looks best when it first comes in the door (or when it is photographed in the catalog), and the veneer finishes and staple-glued joints start to give way after a year or two, depending on how hard you press them.

Years ago I bought what I thought at the time was a beautiful bed frame from Pottery Barn, and when it arrived I was disappointed to find that it looked totally different from the way I'd seen it styled in the catalog. Then, due to the dryness of our apartment, the wood separated on the frame, and for the past four years we have used a variety of wood blocks and the occasional screw to hold the whole thing together. This was not a cheap bed—I remember paying $800 at the time—but by the time we finally replace it, it will be worth nothing, and we will have to throw it out. Not even the Salvation Army will take it away. At an even later point in time, the value of an old bed frame like this will be negative. We might have to pay someone to take it away, as it won't go in the garbage. This bed is a carbohydrate. It provides only short-term sustenance to your home.

Compare with this the bed frame that Jemma and Kevin bought. For about $2,000, their antique Indonesian bed is solid wood with finely crafted joints and tightly fitting slats. This bed, if properly cared for, will only grow in value and will be something they can take with them to every apartment they live in. The value of this piece will be reflected not only in its durable price, but also in the continued enjoyment and service that it gives their home. This bed is a protein. It provides long-term sustenance to their home.

Protein furniture is finely crafted and well made, while carbohydrate furniture is cheaply mass made. As with any diet, both groups are valuable, but a better, more energetic home will cut down on the carbohydrate furniture over time and increase the amount of protein furniture.

When shopping at the bigger retail stores, it is good to know what they do well. Following is a ranking of the stores I use regularly, as well as their specialties:

Crate & Barrel—While their style tends to be safe and not trendsetting, the furniture department is very good. Quality is high and service is excellent. The furniture division is separate from the assemble-it-yourself furniture that Crate & Barrel offers on the first floor.

Design Within Reach—DWR has a great selection of quality midcentury modern and contemporary furniture. Since they are not a manufacturer, prices are higher and shipping has been reported to be very expensive on occasion.

IKEA—IKEA is where you go for basics such as cabinets and shelving, bedding and curtains, tables and desks. These items are excellent for their low price point and will serve well. However, most of IKEA's other pieces won't stand up to heavy use or movement, lighting is unreliable, and glassware breaks easily. In general, at IKEA the more attractive it is, the more quickly it will lose its luster.

West Elm—Started by Pottery Barn for urban dwellers with smaller spaces, West Elm's design is attractive, but their quality is only fair. Beds have been reported extremely unreliable, while their tables are handsome but cheaply made.

Pottery Barn—The biggest of the big, Pottery Barn always looks good, but watch out for quality! I won't go near their furniture, but I rely on their curtains, curtain rods, and rugs, which are all excellent at their lower price point.

Williams-Sonoma Home—This newcomer from the Williams-Sonoma empire is a nice addition, with higher-quality furniture at higher prices. Style is strong but subdued, and quality is excellent.

Be choosy when shopping these stores, and if you do need something beautiful, look at the next rung up. If you can spend a little more to buy something from someone who has actually made it, or something that has been carefully made in small batches from a unique design, this is usually worth it.

Decide on the Total Scope of Work to Be Done. By the end of this week, I want you to look at your vision, your budget, your estimates, and the amount of time you will be able to devote to your one room. Make a reasonable decision as to what you are going to do over the next four weeks and what you will save for a later date. You are making a decision on what the total scope of work is going to be.

As you make this decision, remember two laws of home improvement:

1. Everything is going to take a little longer than you think.
2. Everything is going to cost a little more than you expect.

This is not to say that all of your good work organizing your time and your expenses is not accurate. It is simply that we all share a natural tendency to try to do more than we can, so we consistently underestimate. I do this, clients do it, and even contractors do this. Smart contractors will actually add money and time to a bid just to build in some wiggle room so they don't stress themselves or you in the event that things don't go as planned. This is a smart strategy, and you should be doing the same.

Since I want you to feel successful and since I advocate simplicity above all else, be careful about taking on more than you can reasonably handle in the weeks ahead. As you decide on the total scope of your project, be ambitious, but give yourself some room. Coming in ahead of schedule and under budget is much better than coming in late and over budget.

Consider Hiring a Professional Organizer. Organizing is a relatively new profession, and while I find the term "professional organizer" slightly humorous, it is clear to me that this is a very useful service. I consider organizers temporary personal assistants, and they can be incredibly valuable in helping to facilitate a move, a renovation, or a makeover. I refer organizers regularly to help clients get the ball rolling and do the heavy lifting of sorting or moving papers, files, and furniture into or out of an apartment.

The good thing about organizers is that they are usually energetic, let's-get-it-done-now types of people, but with enough sensitivity not to make you feel overwhelmed. If you are ready to do some work in your apartment and know what you want to do, having an extra pair of eyes and hands around is a real asset.

In keeping with their trade, organizers are a well-organized group and easy to find. The National Association of Professional Organizers can be found online along with listings for organizers in your city (www.napo.net).

Visit a Paint Store This Week to Find Samples. Now is the time to begin to think about color choices if this is going on your list. Choosing the right color to paint your walls is a very easy thing to do if you follow the steps below:

1. Choose five to ten paint samples (chips) at the store.
2. View these at home and reduce selection to your top three choices.
3. Purchase quarts or test bottles of these three colors and paint one-foot-square patches of your wall in at least three different places (in the sun and away from the sun).
4. Allow for viewing over at least one day and night.
5. Choose one of these three.
6. If none works, go back to step 1 and repeat the process until you're successful.

This week, take care of the first step. Stop by your local paint store and select your top five to ten choices for each room you are considering painting.

Choosing colors is fun if you don't feel pressured and are comfortable with experimenting before you commit yourself to painting. It is good to be creative and use your Style Tray for color ideas. If it works in your Style Tray, it will work in your room. You can take photographs from your Style Tray and match them to paint chips, or you can take objects from the room in question and match colors off of those. This is when you need to pay attention to the color world you are creating, and color inspiration can come from anywhere: rugs, lamps, objects, pictures, or even memories.

When looking at colors, feel free to look at those from different companies. I use **Benjamin Moore** paint because it is easy to purchase in New York City, they have a wide selection of colors, and they offer an environmentally sound line of paint called Eco Spec (Eco Spec is not sold in quarts, so I test my colors with regular paint and then buy Eco Spec gallons when I know what I want). **Pratt & Lambert** and Benjamin Moore paints are very popular with interior designers. If you're looking specifically at whites, **Ralph Lauren** has a superior collection. When looking for brilliant, shiny, rich colors, the best on the market is **Schreuder Paints**. While very expensive (about $50 a gallon), these oil-based colors are very durable and useful for small spaces such as backsplashes and closet floors. I am also a big fan of Martha Stewart's line of **Everyday Paints** for Kmart. While the paint is not as high in quality, the prices are affordable and her colors are outstanding. Additionally, **Martha Stewart's Signature Line** of expensive paints (produced with Schreuder) is beautiful and worth looking at for its wide range of earthy and sophisticated neutral colors.

On the high end, **Farrow & Ball** consistently wins rave reviews for their rich colors, which are regularly used in British shelter magazines. Unlike other paint manufacturers, Farrow & Ball mixes more pigment into their colors to create a deeper tone. Recently I have also heard good things about so-called full-spectrum paints, which are rich in pigment, less toxic in their chemistry, and offer a range of colors that seek to match the earth's natural palette. I have not had the opportunity to test them. Much more expensive by the gallon, full-spectrum paints are available from **Citron Paint** (www.citronpaint.com), **Devine Color** (www.devinecolor.com), and **Ellen Kennon Paints** (www.ellenkennon.com).

I like to stick with one company when looking at color chips and will wander into other product lines only if I can't find the color I want. It is also good to know that most paint stores can mix any color from an expensive paint line in a less expensive paint, such as Benjamin Moore.

Chapter Eight

Week Five:
Getting into the
Thick of It

"Ugh!" said Amanda under her breath. "This is endless. What do I do with this? Is this important?"

Amanda had piles of important personal papers that had never been dealt with. They had been stuffed into two cabinets and a drawer since she had lived in her apartment. To tackle the problem, I spent a few days with her sitting on her living room floor sifting through piles of paper. They went back three to four years, ever since she had graduated from college.

Going through the messy piles, most of the paperwork fell easily into typical categories such as "bank statements," "retirement account," or "personal letters," but we kept coming across strange scraps of paper, photographs, drawings, and small objects that made Amanda laugh and quickly turn them facedown.

"What's this one?" I would ask.

"Oh, that's from my sweetie," she would say, laughing and quickly taking it out of my hands.

Eventually we were done, but there was this sizable stack of assorted papers that had no home. They were all from her "sweetie."

"Amanda, can we put those in the Outbox now?"

"Absolutely not!"

"Well, if you keep these things, they have to have a proper home. You need to honor them. I want you to make a file for all of it and give the file a name."

Amanda consented and arranged all the papers and odds and ends into two large files that then went into one hanging folder. The problem then was that she had no name for the files.

I made a few suggestions. "How about 'boyfriend'?"

"No."

" 'Memories'?"

"No way."

" 'Personal'?"

"No."

"How about 'sweetie'?"

Amanda laughed. She liked the idea. After all, that was

the one word that summed up this collection. After she started the Sweetie File, it grew in size and became her favorite reason for going into her files and keeping them in order.

Week Five: Deep Treatment

Bones
Take care of repairs this week.
Clean office area and related closets.
Vacuum, dust, and mop throughout.

Breath
Declutter files.
Tackle the cord octopus.
Try a one-day media fast.

Heart
Buy fresh flowers.
Choose at least one soft or hard thing to add or subtract.

Head
Cook three meals at home this week.
Eat at home Sunday through Thursday.
Get to bed early and read before sleep.
Optional: look into wireless technology.

Week Five: One-Room Remedy

Order from your Shopping List.
Try paint samples in the room.
Finalize paint choices.

Deep Treatment

Bones

Take Care of Repairs This Week. This is just a reminder to make sure that all of your repairs are getting taken care of. Since repairs are often necessary before decorative work can take place, these should be done first. At this point you have this week and next week remaining to check off everything on your Repair Worksheet.

Clean Office Area and Related Closets. Clean up and around your office and all related storage areas. For some people, this will be a separate room, while for others it may be the corner of the living room or dining room. Clean it out! With vacuum, spray bottle, and wet rag, get behind and on top of shelves. Move objects and clean behind them, and get everything out of any related closets so that these can be cleaned as well. Note the improvements you want for this room, and try your hand at just one of them this week.

Vacuum, Dust, and Mop Throughout. Since four weeks have passed, it is time to do a deeper cleaning of all floors and surfaces. Pass through each room, cleaning all the floors and dusting any surfaces such as cabinets, tables, and windowsills.

If your vacuum is hard to reach or not easy to use and you find yourself resisting using it, store it differently and/or consider replacing it. Cleaning should be made as easy as possible. You should be able to roll your vacuum out of a closet with one hand and in one motion. If it takes more than this, it is too difficult.

Breath

Declutter Files. Home office files and papers are among the most vexing clutter problems in the home. Personal finances are often the worst. Paper clutter accumulates when decisions about what the best action to take are deferred. When you find yourself thinking, "I'll decide that later" or "I'll just hold on to it for now," and you don't have a plan of action for when that will be, clutter is going to follow. Don't put off these decisions.

Keeping on top of paperwork and filing is the only way to make it easier and keep important issues from becoming urgent. The secret here is not to file too much and to establish regular windows of time to focus on and make decisions in this area.

The Birth of Files

Most papers that make their way to the home office start life as mail coming through the front door. If you have your Landing Strip sorting process set up, you will have already won half of the battle. At your front door, you should have a dedicated slot for all bills, financial statements, and any business-related mail that requires a response. You should keep all of this important mail by your front door until you are ready to act on it.

Establish the day or days on which you pay bills. I pay bills each week; some people pay them biweekly; most pay them monthly. Choose the timing that is best for you and put it on your calendar. It is important that this date with yourself becomes a ritual that occurs like clockwork.

Use Your Boundaries to Make It Easier

One of my clients deals with all billing, both personal and professional, on Wednesdays, and doesn't look at bills or think about them until then. He uses this carefully boundaried time to deal with the intricacies of bill paying and making financial decisions, but also as a way of keeping those tasks out of the rest of his time. If anyone asks him about insurance, a donation, or a bill that needs to be paid, he makes a note of it and says he will take a look at it on Wednesday. Financial commitments can get urgent and at times can unnecessarily press in upon you. Organizing them not only in a basket by the door but also in a regular window of time will allow you to say no to others when necessary and ensure that you have the space to make good decisions.

Paying Bills at the Office

Many of my friends and clients who have a lot of bills to pay do so at the office at the end of the day or over a lunch hour. This means that they do not have bills and financial statements piling up at home, but take them off the Landing Strip each day and bring them to the office. If you have limited space at home and your office is relaxed enough to accommodate this, I recommend it. Taking care of personal bills at the office is a good way of taking pressure off your apartment and keeping your home office needs to a minimum.

What to Keep, What to Throw Out

When you sit down to deal with your finances, the goal should be to meet all of your commitments, plan ahead, and keep the minimum amount of paper. This makes it easier to store important documents and find them when you need them. The papers that make files grow the quickest are the many pages of monthly telephone and utility bills (gas, electric, cell phone, etc.), so I would advise against keeping them at all unless they are business expenses. Following is a list of what you should keep and for how long:

Keep:	**For How Long:**
1. Personal letters	Permanently
2. Tax returns	Permanently
3. Credit card statements	Seven years
4. Mortgage statements	Seven years
5. Bank statements	Seven years
6. Investment statements	Seven years (keep first statement for life of investment)
7. Loose deductible business receipts	Seven years
8. Deductible business bills	Seven years
9. Insurance policies	Three years of renewals
10. Warranties, user's guides	Life of product

Do not keep:

1. Personal or holiday cards
2. Utility bills (unless deductible)

3. Rent receipts
4. Nondeductible receipts or bills

The primary reason for holding on to financial records is so that you can keep track of your expenses and double-check whenever there is any doubt about a payment. The secondary reason for holding on to your records is in case of an IRS audit. In both cases, seven years is more than enough time for holding on to most records and will keep you completely safe with the IRS, who can audit six years of your financial records if they feel you have un-derreported income by 25 percent.

If you have complicated finances or are particularly ea-ger to keep longer-term records, I recommend that you use a program such as **Quicken, Quickbooks,** or **Money** to record your checks and deposits and run reports. This will allow you to keep detailed notes on all your expenses for as long as you want without having to keep the paper at all.

Keeping Files Organized

Keeping your files clearly marked and organized will make your life easier. This is another case where the ini-tial investment of a little time pays big dividends. If you don't have these items already, I recommend purchasing:

1. Hanging file folders
2. Colored tab files (a different color for each area of your life)
3. A labeler

These three things will make your files easy to locate and use. There is nothing worse than a tightly cramped file drawer with worn-down little tabs that you can barely read. Color-coding the basic areas of your life and then labeling them with black letters on a white background is a tremendous help. Here is an example of one of Amanda's file drawers:

1. Personal: pink folders
   a. Creative
      i. Personal projects
      ii. Travel plans
      iii. Cooking
   b. Personal letters
      i. Family
      ii. Sweetie
      iii. Friends
   c. Business
      i. Bank statement
      ii. Credit card statement
      iii. Mortgage statement
      iv. Retirement account
      v. Investment statement
      vi. Health insurance
      vii. Home insurance
   d. Photographs
2. Professional: green folders
   a. Creative
      i. Story ideas
      ii. Rough drafts
      iii. Final clips
   b. Business
      i. Business credit card statement
      ii. Current deductible receipts
      iii. Past deductible receipts
3. Household warranties, etc.: orange folders

Tackle the Cord Octopus. As with paperwork, the cords that we now need to power and connect our computers, telephones, printers, and faxes grow wild over time. This is your week to straighten this out if it has become a mess. Here are some tips:

1. Avoid using too many cables, and remove any unused ones that may be floating around your floor. Also, remove any peripheral devices that you don't use (do you really use your printer or can you print things out at the office?) and go wireless where you can.

2. Keep your devices as close together as possible and use the shortest cords you can so that excess cord doesn't accumulate.

3. Tightly bind cords into one central cable with cord managers. For this you want a cord manager that you can easily remove. The best kind is the flexible coil that tightly wraps around the cable. My favorites are **Cleverline Cable Managers** from The Container Store and Cable organizer.com (both of these shops have other excellent solutions as well).

4. Tack up all cables that run along the wall with an **Arrow T-25 staple gun**. This gun is made especially for stapling around wires and cords and will not harm them.

Try a One-Day Media Fast. This idea was inspired by Dr. Andrew Weil's *Eight Weeks to Optimum Health*. It is simple and powerful, and I have introduced it to many clients.

Since the goal of the Eight-Week Cure is to reclaim your home and to reduce the pressures and stimulation of the outside world, another culprit to be aware of is the ubiquitous media: television, radio, and newspapers. Dr. Weil calls his fast a "news fast" and says not to read, watch, or listen to any news for a full day. He then goes on to explain why:

> *I do not want you to become uninformed about the state of the world, but I note that paying attention to news commonly results in anxiety, rage, and other emotional states that probably impede the healing system. . . . I think that it is useful to broaden the concept of nutrition to include what we put into our consciousness as well. Many people do not exercise much control over that and as a result take in a lot of mental junk food. My goal is for you to discover that you have the power to decide how much of this material you want to let in.*

I have found Dr. Weil's approach to be both wise and effective; however, I do not feel it goes far enough. Many of my clients have a television in the middle of their living room that is turned on the moment they come home and runs all evening. Whereas Dr. Weil calls simply for a "news fast," I have found that a media fast is now needed to remove the mental junk food that I find in most homes. Therefore, avoid the television during your workday and turn it off completely while you are at home. If your work makes this impossible for you during the week, try this on the weekend. (While playing music at home is fine, if you want to go further, try turning this off as well.)

As you experience your day, and especially your home time, without the usual sights and sounds to listen to, pay attention to how you feel. While you may find it uncomfortable and unfamiliar at first, you will inevitably find yourself with time that is unfilled and now yours to spend in new ways.

I have received tremendous affirmation from clients and Apartment Therapy readers that this is a valuable exercise. One e-mail I received from a woman in Chicago said that she started doing this with her husband one night a week and it became her favorite night at home. She found that she and her husband spoke with each other and did things together that they never did on other nights when the television was on. She wrote that she wished that every night was like this, but that it would be impossible for her husband to turn the television off that much.

Heart

Buy Fresh Flowers. As you continue to buy fresh flowers, experiment with where you find them and what kind you buy, and get to know what their names are. Consider it your weekly mission to learn the names of three new flowers or other plants. If it is during the warmer months and you have the opportunity to bring fresh flowers back from the country, try this instead.

Observe how your home feels and how it is to come home each evening. Is it refreshing to see flowers when you walk in your door? Does it make you happy? Which kinds do you like? Do people comment on them? Does the fresh color make the room livelier?

By adding a living element, you are doing something that is very personal and symbolic in honoring your home. When you get to the end of the Eight-Week Cure, you will then decide how important this has been and how often you will keep it up.

Choose at Least One Soft or Hard Thing to Add or Subtract. Last week you looked at the hardness or softness in each room of your home. This week identify what you need to balance the softness in each room and choose at least one thing to change, through either removal or addition. If you want to take something away, move it to the Outbox. If you need to add a soft element, try a pillow, rug, or set of curtains. If you need to add a hard element, try a glass side table, a metal or ceramic lamp, or even a framed photograph.

After you have done this, observe how this has affected the room. Was it uncomfortable for you to do? Does it make the room any different? Can you sense the interplay of hard and soft, mineral and organic in your home?

As you notice this balance you may find yourself adding or subtracting more. I want you to begin to see each room as an instrument that can be tuned to strike the most comfortable and invigorating note.

Head

Cook Three Meals at Home This Week. Judy and Chuck order in most nights, and so does Marlo. Another client, Nathan, told me he had cooked at home three times in the three years he had lived there. While okay in the short term, not using the home kitchen is one of the leading causes of "apartment death" in the city.

Your apartment serves three primary functions that have been the role of our homes ever since early humans dragged themselves out of the rain and into their first cave: shelter from the elements, a place to cook, and a way to keep warm. At first the hearth was a fire, then it was a fireplace, then it became a stove; now it is in danger of existing only in the bright flicker of the television. Many

SUNDAY NIGHT 101

4:00 p.m.: Head out on foot and shop for dinner

Sunday is the traditional day for a roast, and the simple recipe for roast chicken with vegetables is an easy and delicious place to start if you have no other ideas. Don't buy prepared food; be sure that you do the roasting. Buy good, organic ingredients and spoil yourself with a nice cheese and dessert as well. Don't limit yourself to just shopping for dinner, either. Take this time to stock your fridge for the week with basic ingredients such as juice, butter, milk, or pasta.

Buy good food. For much less money than you spend eating out, you can buy gourmet food and ingredients to stock your home. Treating yourself to food you like will provide you with an extra incentive to eat at home.

This is also a good time to purchase flowers for your table or bedroom.

5:00 p.m.: Get home and clean up

After a busy week, you may have to clean up your apartment in order to get cooking. Good. This is part of what it is all about. Clean up the kitchen, change your sheets, do laundry, take out the garbage. Using your home is the best way to keep it in fine shape, and if you take no other time in the week, then this one day will do. The goal here is to make it comfortable and fresh for the week ahead. With the television off tonight, put on some music instead.

6:00 p.m.: Start cooking

Depending on how much cleaning you have to do or if there are one or two of you at home, cooking could start later or sooner. The important thing is to begin early. An early dinner on Sunday night helps calm down your system and allows you to go to bed earlier. After a late night on Friday and Saturday, you don't want to go to bed late again.

Whether you are cooking by yourself or with a partner, you are now deep in "home time." This is when you review your weekend and the week past and think about what you want to do in the week ahead. While you chop vegetables or sauté garlic, you are giving yourself space to let the dust settle, fold up all the rumpled clothes of your mind, and refocus on what is important to you.

If one of you is cooking and the other not, this is a good time to share a glass of wine with a tasty cheese and crackers while you talk. This is also a good time to call your family (but not if they drive you crazy) or for one of you to write short thank-yous to people from the past week. This is not about simply putting food on the table; it is about heightening domestic enjoyment.

7:00 p.m.: Sit down to dinner

Sitting down to a home-cooked meal is a ritual that will enrich you even if you are eating by yourself. If you are alone, read something that you haven't had time for all week. And don't sit on the couch! Eat in your dining room (even if it is only a small table on the side of your living room) or at your studio's island counter.

The richest, most satisfying part of the evening comes when you bite into food that you have cooked. There is nothing quite like a home-cooked meal, and if you doubt your skill in the kitchen, Sunday night is a good time to experiment with new recipes and ingredients. Even cooking spaghetti can become a gourmet experiment.

8:00 p.m.: Clean up and go for a walk

If you have done a good job, you have cooked more than enough food and have some delicious leftovers for the week ahead.

Cleaning up is important. You don't want to wake in the morning to dirty dishes of any kind, so clean everything and put everything away. Scrub down all the surfaces, including your dining table, and throw out any old food in your fridge before you put left-overs away.

Head out for a walk. Getting out and moving after a meal is good for digestion and another way to clear your mind and give yourself time to talk or think about what is going on in your life. Between partners this is another time to talk about problems or worries and iron them out if you haven't done so already.

9:00 p.m.: Get ready for bed with a book

Getting to bed early on Sunday night will ensure a successful week. You will be up early, rested, and ready for whatever work or madness comes your way. If, like I do, you have a hard time falling asleep at night (especially on Sunday, when your body has become used to staying up later), try hot herbal tea and reading in bed. If you have more difficulty, a hot bath will soothe and calm your muscles, and melatonin pills are a safe, natural way of inducing drowsiness if used once a week.

Home time is about rejuvenation, and reading at the end of the day is a big part of this (don't make it work-related). If there is nothing you can think of reading, get a classic and dive in. Reading a good book, especially fiction, is an expansive act that allows your mind to leave the cares of the week and occupy a higher plane, accompanied by the inspiration of others.

9:30 p.m.: Lights out

Sound impossibly early? It won't feel early if you have eaten early and done everything else on this list. This is a big night at home, and you will find yourself pleasantly tired and looking forward to the next day.

Again, using your home is the best way to take care of it. In taking these hours at home, you have touched on almost every part of your apartment, strengthening both the foundation of your home and the foundation of your own person. You and your home are nourished, rested, and prepared.

people keep the television on for emotional warmth, eat in front of it, and allow it to be the center of their apartment. As you turn off your television this week, restore the true hearth by using Sunday night to cook at home.

Sunday night is the most important night to cook at home and by far the sweetest once you get into the habit. It is the easiest to plan for, since many of us are so busy that it is hard to count on being home for dinner any other night of the week. Sunday is the quiet day before your busy week begins and the best time to check in with yourself, your partner, or your family. This is the night to prepare for the week ahead and nourish yourself and your home in the process. And among other things, cooking at home on Sunday nights is a sure cure for those people who get the Sunday blues.

Eat at Home Sunday Through Thursday. This week you are going to extend the nights you eat at home to the five weeknights. This gets you into a good rhythm with plenty of home time. Cooking can be light on a number of nights as you heat up leftovers, but try adding a fresh vegetable or a new spice to your dishes so that each night you try something new.

These are not evenings for entertaining friends at home. They are primarily for making sure that you are staying on top of the projects you are working on in your home. Since this week involves sorting out your files, finalizing paint choices, and building your Shopping List so that you will be ready to purchase what you need next week, you have plenty to do.

Most of my clients and people I know do not spend this much time each week cooking and eating at home. If this is also true of you, observe the changes and opportunities that it creates in your week. Do you find yourself leaving work earlier? Do you look forward to the activities you have planned at home? Does it bore you? Do you feel differently about your home as you leave it in the morning?

Among other things, you should find that you are more in touch with your apartment's vital signs: you know what is needed in the refrigerator, the paint that is drying in the bedroom is on your mind, or you remember to move the furniture away from the wall so that the super can fix the broken outlet. For the next four weeks you are going to keep your home time at this level, allowing you to give full attention to the Cure and see what happens when you make this kind of investment in your home. Afterward, it will be up to you to see if you want to keep to this schedule or modify it.

Get to Bed Early and Read Before Sleep. As with the Sunday program, I want you to make every attempt to get to bed early on weeknights this month. As Dr. Weil says in *Eight Weeks to Optimum Health,* "Adequate sleep is a key element of a healthy lifestyle; lack of it increases susceptibility to illness." Not only is sleep important, but allowing yourself time in bed in the evening and time to get ready in the morning is one of life's great domestic luxuries. Rushing into or out of bed and clipping your day at the beginning and end will not allow you to take the small moments that are necessary for paying attention to your home. As sleep marks both the end and the beginning of the day, start to think about being early on both fronts, not late or even on time.

Optional: Look into Wireless Technology. Many of the advances in media technology in the past twenty years have had a dubious impact on the home. As the role of media in our lives has grown and we have figured out more and more ways to turn our homes into video arcades and movie theaters, we have brought more electronics into our home than ever before. Electronic stimulation is not good for the home, and I recommend keeping it to a minimum as well as finding ways of keeping it out of sight.

However, two technological advances have become available to homeowners in the past few years that I fully approve of: wireless routers (or Wi-Fi) working over a high-speed connection and the ability to store all of your music on your computer.

Many of my clients have laptops at home, which require being tethered to an Ethernet cable in order to hook up to the Internet via DSL or cable modem. This means that they are forced to sit in one part of their apartment when online. In these cases, I recommend a wireless router (about $60), which allows you to get rid of the cable hookup and work or browse from any room in your home. If technology is to be useful, it should give us mobility, not tie us down, and this is exactly what wireless networks do. Installing a wireless router with a high-speed modem or DSL line is extremely simple, and on the occasions when I have had to call for technical assistance, I have been helped quickly by both of the wireless router companies I have purchased from (**D-Link** and **LinkSys**).

With the wireless hub and another device, such as **Apple's AirPort Express** or **Slim Devices' Squeezebox,** you are also able to play music from your computer wirelessly from any room in your apartment. This requires a certain amount of nerdiness, but it is getting easier and easier to do, and no one that I know who has tried it, client or friend, has ever gone back.

One-Room Remedy

Order from Your Shopping List. You are halfway through, and you have done a great deal. You have built a vision, set a budget, researched, and put your project in motion. You may have worked with a floor plan and started choosing paint colors. You should have collected estimates on what everything will cost or should be finishing that up this week. The list may be big and include a painter, contractor, paint, new curtains, and a new kitchen floor, or it may be small and only include a few cans of paint, two pillows, and this book. Whatever you have chosen to include in your project, make sure that the following holds true: consider this an investment in your home, not simply your apartment; invest in quality, not quantity; don't buy anything you don't love, need, and have room for; don't buy anything cheap; and if you are unsure of something, leave it off the list.

This week, make sure that everything you are thinking of buying is on your list. Here is an example of what it should look like:

Project: Living Room Makeover
Budget: $8,500
Theme: Contemporary, Clean, Relaxing
Style: Modern Organic

Room/Item	#	Description	Estimated Price	Store	Actual Price	Done	Delivery Date & Notes
Living Room							
sofa	1	wood, mid-century modern, MaterialDesign.com	$1,500				
coffee table	1		$300				
small armchair or ottoman	1	slipper chairs	$500				
rug, 6x9	2	Bubbles – Crate & Barrel	$500				
floor lamps (by couch)	2		$300				
media stand	1		$200				
curtain panels	2		$45				
curtain rod	1		$25				
side table	1		$50				
table lamp	1		$150				
uplights	2		$50				
radio controller	1		$30				
		total	**$3,650**				
Labor							
carpentry		remove shelving, install shelving, curtains - 4 days @ $350	$1,400				
flooring		refinish and stain main floor - 222 sq ft @ $3 per sq foot	$800				
painting		2 days at $225	$450				
paint			$100				
Incidentals*			$250				
		subtotal	**$6,650**	subtotal	$0		
		tax @ 8.625%	$574	delivery	$0		
		delivery	$200	**Grand Total**	**$0**		
		Incidentals @ 5%	$333				
		Grand Total	**$7,757**				

Purchasing

If you have a small Shopping List, it should be easy to get things purchased this week, but if you have a bigger list, double-check everything and make sure you have all the information you need to be organized around this significant expenditure of your money. Here are a few tips on purchasing:

BRINGING IN NEW ITEMS

When you have spent a great deal of time weeding, you become very careful with what you plant.

Be very conscious of the new items that you bring into your home. With all the care you are taking to create good energy in your apartment, you don't want to relapse with an impulse buy or a filler to help out a situation while you look for what would be perfect. Avoid buying on impulse.

The greatest discovery you can make at this point is feeling a new desire to cut down on what had been your previous approach to purchasing. I have had many clients who, after a great deal of Outboxing and cleaning, surprise themselves by purchasing very little. I have had others say to me that they have found themselves becoming very picky, not wanting to ruin what they have done. This is good. Don't be afraid of leaving a space empty if you don't find the thing you are looking for. An empty space is easier to maintain and always has potential.

1. Purchase everything on the same day.
2. Write down final prices.
3. Write down delivery estimates.
4. Double-check each order (model number, fabric, etc.).
5. Use a credit card.

Purchasing generates a lot of information, and you want to be sure that you keep it all together. Purchasing everything you need in one day helps you to do this, and using a credit card is a good way not only of collecting some benefit (air miles, etc.), but also of ensuring that if there is a dispute or your order is botched, you have someone else on your side to help get your money back.

Out of Stock?

You may also find that after careful research, what you want is out of stock, delayed, or not quite what you thought it was. Don't let this throw you off. This happens all the time. On jobs with clients, I find that there are always last-minute shuffles to be dealt with and that these can often open up new opportunities to be creative.

Necessity is the mother of invention. Many of the solutions I have come up with at the last minute have been the best. For example, if you plan to buy off-white silk curtains at a certain store but suddenly find that they are out of stock, take a look at the other colors that are similar, or other fabrics in the color you like. Despite the fact that you have been set on silk, a linen curtain may be even better. If when you get to the hardware store you can't find the piece of hardware you are looking for, ask for help and describe the project. The store may have a different, better, or easier solution that you don't know about.

You may be surprised at how quickly you sort through other options and come up with a new solution. In cases where things are delayed, I recommend you put your order through and look around for another option at the same time. In cases where you can't quite decide between two things and you are easily able to return one to the store, I recommend that you buy both to try out in your home.

Try Paint Samples in the Room. Having chosen three colors you like, buy these in quarts or test cans this week. You are now at the second step in the decision-making process. Using a brush and being careful not to drip, paint two or three one-foot-square patches on your walls in areas near and far from any windows. With a pencil, lightly mark next to each patch which paint color is which, and let dry.

Over the next twenty-four hours take the time to look at the different colors in the daylight and at night under lamplight. Colors change dramatically depending on the light, and only now do you have the best representation of how the color will actually look on the wall when the whole thing is painted.

Looking at what you have on the wall, choose the one you like the best. If none of these seems right, be patient and start with paint chips again. You will find that unlike the first round, you know a lot more than you did, and you will surely find the color you like this time around.

Meg's Moroccan Inspiration

Meg had just returned from Morocco with a desire to infuse her apartment with colors from North Africa. For the reupholstering of her couch and chairs, she chose fabric that matched the bright colors of a dress she had brought back from her trip, but she was unsure about what to do on the walls. Bright colors on the walls didn't seem like a good idea, as she wanted to keep her apartment light and bright. Drawing on what a friend had done in her apartment, and looking hard at her Style Tray, Meg decided that the right balance for all the colors that she liked was a neutral: the light, sandy colors of the desert.

Within days, she had several different off-whites painted in squares on her walls, and in a few more days she had even more. Looking at all these samples, she couldn't decide. To make it easier we did two things: we painted the swatches next to door frames, where the color would be seen against the trim of her doors, and repainted the patches larger on top of white squares of primer. The white background made it easier to see the color, as it wasn't affected by the preexisting color.

The white framing allowed Meg to see the subtleties between the different colors more easily, and her fears and indecisiveness retreated. Her next problem was that she liked too many of the colors. In the end, Meg decided to keep many of the colors by painting every room a different shade.

Meg was choosing between off-whites, which can be hard. Here are a few tips to make it easier:

1. Paint large patches against corners and door frames.
2. Paint them on top of pure white primer if the existing color of the wall is too strong or too close to the one you are testing.
3. Paint a whole section of a wall from floor to ceiling if you are really stumped.
4. View off-whites in daylight.

Choosing colors can be very hard, especially because color interacts with anything near it. Isolating colors from one another always helps.

Finalize Paint Choices. Choose one color to move forward with. It should match the room in terms of coolness or warmth, and it should pull out some of the colors that are already in the room. It should also be represented in your Style Tray.

When you have found the right color for your walls, it often becomes necessary to consider a color and type of paint for other surfaces as well. Here are a few words on what to do with ceilings and trim, as well as how to choose primer and the finish of your paint.

Trim

First of all, what is trim? Trim was traditionally the finishing pieces of woodwork that protected walls and corners from damage. These raised pieces received the heaviest use from shoes, chairs, and hands and needed a finish that was easy to clean and repair. The following is considered trim: baseboards along the bottom of walls, molding around doorways and windows, doors themselves, and window frames. Traditional architecture includes a lot of trim, while Modern architecture considers it superfluous and has very little. Whatever type of space you live in, painting the trim will affect the style. Here are some tips for choosing trim colors.

Modern Look—For a Modern look, hide the trim by painting it the same color as the wall and toning down the finish with eggshell or semigloss.

Traditional Look—For a Traditional look, highlight the trim by painting it a different color. Bright white will give it a fresh look, while using a darker tone of the wall color will give it an old-fashioned look. Using a bright color against a white wall will imitate the early Shaker style.

Ceilings

All ceilings should be whiter than the walls. There should be a line of difference where the walls end and the ceiling begins. They should, therefore, be painted white with a color such as Decorator's White or Ceiling White. These are standard whites for use on ceilings. They have just a touch of color in them, so they are not reflective or too bright, but they will stand out from the color you put on your walls.

Primer

Is primer necessary? To be honest, I rarely use it, but that is because few rooms I encounter require it. I consider primer necessary if the color you are painting over is very dark or if there are stains on the wall that will show through. It is also necessary to create a more receptive surface if you are using latex paint on a wall that was covered previously with enamel or has been newly repaired with spackle and tape.

In general, unless the room you are painting really needs help in its bone structure, three coats of latex paint will do the job just fine.

Nontoxic Paints and Finishes

If you want a wake-up call that points out how important it is to keep your home healthy and consume carefully, listen to this: indoor air is three times more polluted than outdoor air and is considered one of the top five hazards to human health by the EPA. Even more surprising, paints and finishes are among the largest contributors to indoor air pollution.

To combat this and to comply with new environmental regulations and consumer demand, paint companies have begun to produce natural, low-VOC, and zero-VOC paints, which reduce the amount of volatile organic compounds (VOCs) released into your home. If you would like to know much more about the subject, the following Web sites offer a great deal of information along with recommendations:

Eartheasy.com
Greenseal.org
Watoxics.org (Washington Toxics Coalition)

But while using healthier paints makes overwhelming sense, finding the colors you want can be difficult. Healthier paints tend to have a more limited color range compared to regular commercial brands. They can also be harder to find, though more and more are available online.

Following are paints that I have used or heard good things about, and recommend:

Benjamin Moore Pristine Eco Spec Paints (low-VOC)
Sherwin Williams New Harmony Paints (zero-VOC)
EcoDesign's BioShield paints and finishes (natural)
Livos paints and finishes (natural)

Aglaia Paints (natural)
Old Fashioned Milk Paint Company (natural)

It is worth considering using these paints, especially if you want to support the manufacture of products that are better for our homes, our families, and our earth.

Flat, Semigloss, or Gloss?

Flat paint is standard for walls. This is the finish I recommend most for living spaces. It is a general-purpose finish that hides imperfections. Flat's matte finish also sits back in a room, highlighting your furniture and showing its own color in a very rich and saturated way. However, flat absorbs moisture and picks up dirt easily, which takes it out of the running for bathrooms or high-use surfaces such as door frames and bookshelves.

Eggshell can be used on walls that are in good shape. Eggshell's slight sheen gives it a fancier appearance that some people prefer and is easier to clean, but it will show imperfections more easily. It can be used in larger bathrooms, as it is somewhat resistant to humidity.

Semigloss is for general trim. Easy to wipe down and not so shiny that you can see yourself in it, this is the standard finish for door frames, baseboards, and kitchen backsplashes. In small bathrooms where moisture buildup is an issue, semigloss is needed on walls, as eggshell will wrinkle and peel.

Gloss or high-gloss is standard for floors (though it is occasionally used on very-high-end, perfectly smooth walls). High-gloss's tough skin and protective quality make it much longer-lasting and the easiest to clean. I have used it successfully on ugly closet floors as well as on other floors around the house for a light, bright, colorful feeling.

How Much Paint Do I Need?

How many gallons you will need is easy to estimate. Measure your walls by height and width and multiply to find the square footage. You will need one gallon of paint to cover between 400 and 450 square feet. Remember that if you are doing more than one coat you will need to double or triple this.

Once you know how much you need, order your paint. Many stores can take a long time to mix up an order, and you don't want to stand around the store waiting all day. I recommend calling your order in to your nearest paint store and paying over the phone with a credit card. If you order at the end of the day, most stores will mix the paint first thing in the morning and have it ready by 9 a.m.

Chapter Nine

Week Six:
Light Therapy

"I want this room to really pop!"

I was standing with Jeffrey, a lawyer, in the living room of his prewar one-bedroom apartment just off Gramercy Park in a very fancy part of town. He'd been working on his apartment for a while and needed help with only one thing.

"When you walk into the apartment right now, it's sort of blah," he said. "I want people to walk in and be really impressed."

"What ideas have you had?"

"I thought about a really big picture over the sofa and getting some color in here somewhere, but I don't feel comfortable deciding on it alone. I would really like your opinion."

"Well, if you ask me, those aren't bad ideas, but what the room really needs is more light."

"You mean another lamp or something like that?"

"More than that. First of all, I would never use the overhead ceiling fixture that is on right now because it washes out the room, and I would add one lamp to the hallway, two more to the living room area, and one on the dining table at the end of the room."

"Wow, four more lights. That's a lot. Is it really that dark?"

I turned off the overhead. Without this light, it was. Jeffrey had only one table lamp in this living room, while the hall, living area, and kitchen were all lit by ceiling fixtures that cast a dull glow.

"If you really want your rooms to pop, the thing that will do it best is light. Bright colors and beautiful objects won't amount to anything unless they have good light. Right now you've got no real light to even make things pop."

"I see what you mean. I guess I've just gotten used to the lighting the way it is."

"Most people do," I told him. "Most apartments I visit are underlit. We get used to it so quickly that we don't notice it anymore."

A month later, I visited Jeffrey again. This time he had done some shopping.

"You were totally right," he said. "Check out the hallway."

As I walked in, I saw that Jeffrey had placed a bright red table lamp on the hall table directly in front of me. Along with the color in the lamp, the warm light shone on the rich coffee-colored stain of the hall table and accented the off-white on the walls.

"Aside from the fact that lighting was more expensive than I thought, it really makes a difference. All the colors are really popping."

"What about your friends? Have any of them come over and made any comments?"

"Oh, yeah. Everyone who has come over has noticed the difference right when they come in the door. A few have even called my apartment 'sexy,' which is amazingly cool. I had no idea that just adding light would do it."

Week Six: Deep Treatment

Bones
Clean bathrooms and related closets.

Breath
Declutter cabinets and closets.
Arrange your bathroom efficiently.

Heart
Upgrade your razor and shaving supplies.
Purchase bath salts and a nice soap.
Place a candle in your bathroom.
Consider scents for your home.

Head
Plan for the week ahead on Sunday.
Wake early and take a bath before work.
Optional: consider a media fast for the next week.
Optional: straighten your desk at work.

Week Six: One-Room Remedy

Finalize your lighting arrangement.
Get painting.

Deep Treatment

Bones

Clean Bathrooms and Related Closets. Cleaning a bathroom is a fairly straightforward task. You want to make sure that the tub, sink, and toilet are cleaned along with all tile surfaces and the floor, but it is easy not to go deep enough. Here are a few tips to follow:

1. Vinyl shower curtains can be washed in the machine with towels and a bit of bleach.
2. Pour 1 cup of vinegar and ¼ cup of baking soda down the tub drain and let sit for thirty minutes to keep the drain clear.
3. Use an old toothbrush with cleanser to clean the grout between tiles.
4. Wash faucets and taps and dry with a paper towel for an ultimate shine.
5. Recommended cleaners
    a. Toxic/heavy duty
        i.   **Kaboom**
        ii. **Softscrub**
        iii. **Clorox Cleanup**
    b. Nontoxic, biodegradable/heavy duty
        i.   Vinegar and water
        ii. **Bon Ami**
        iii. **Dr. Bronner's Sal Suds**

iv. **Seventh Generation Bathroom Cleaner**
v. Bathroom cleaners by **Caldrea, BioKleen, Ecover,** or **Method**

The bathroom is a heavily used room; it will need not only cleaning but repairs and replacement more often than other rooms. This week you will replace dirty curtains, worn toothbrushes, and wobbly shelves.

One particularly useful invention that I also recommend is rolling shower curtain hooks. These small, indispensable wonders are metal hooks that run on ball bearings and make it much easier to pull your shower curtain open and closed.

Breath

Declutter Cabinets and Closets. Bathroom cabinets are one of the most common places in the home for clutter to develop. Old cold medicine and aftershave can sit unused and forgotten for years in these cabinets. This is your week to clean them all out.

Going through your cabinets, remove anything that meets any of these criteria:

1. You haven't used it in twelve months.
2. It's expired.
3. The container is nearly empty.
4. You don't need it any longer.

Make sure that everything in your cabinets comes out first before you put stuff back in. If you need to use the Outbox, go ahead; otherwise go straight to the garbage.

Arrange Your Bathroom Efficiently. It is easy to over-look the bathroom; it's the smallest room in the home, and many tend to use it very quickly in the morning and evening. However, this week I want you to pay attention to it and see what improvements can be made so that it is easier to use. Here are some suggestions:

1. Does your shower curtain open easily? If not, install curtain hooks with rollers.
2. Are you happy with the shower nozzle? Installing a larger nozzle or massaging shower attachment can make a big difference in your morning shower routine.
3. Is it easy to reach your shampoos? Get these bottles off the tub and into a hanging wire caddy for ease of use.
4. Men: do you like to shave in the shower? Getting a nonfogging shower mirror is a great help.

In general, I want you to strip your bathroom down, keeping products out of sight and putting everything where you most need to use it. If this requires getting another storage rack, then do it now.

Heart

Upgrade Your Razor and Shaving Supplies. While luxuries such as expensive furniture and bigger apartments are not available to all of us, small luxuries in the home should not be overlooked. Whether you are a man or woman, having a nice razor and shaving supplies makes life easier and is better for your skin. Upgrade your razor and supplies this week.

I recommend **Gillette** razors for both men and women, as I believe they are the best-designed and most effective razors available. As for shaving cream, a little goes a long way. Avoid large cans of cream. Tubes of shaving cream or small cans of gel work better and take up less space in the bathroom.

Purchase Bath Salts and a Nice Soap. If you are not in the habit of soaking with bath salts or buying fine soap, do so this week. Look for natural, perfume-free salts and soap. Remember, the soap you buy will be used each and every day to wash your body, so be sure that you buy a bar that makes you feel good.

Place a Candle in Your Bathroom. Find a candle this week for your bathroom. It may be naturally scented or unscented. Having a candle in your bathroom adds a sense of calm to this busy space and will allow you to turn off the lights when you soak in the tub. When I have guests over to dinner, I always leave the light off but keep a candle burning so that they can see their way in.

Consider Scents for Your Home. Artificially scented candles, room fresheners, and potpourri should *not* be in your home, but some natural scents can be. Burning incense can be a very pleasing way of changing the mood or simply masking stale air in the midst of winter, when it is too cold to open your windows (I recommend **Juniper Ridge** incense from www.juniperridge.com). In particular, adding a scented candle to your bathroom can be very practical. Here are some tips when shopping:

1. Check the label carefully to make sure it is natural.
2. Avoid heavy or strong scents.
3. Don't buy cheap candles, as they won't burn as cleanly.
4. Beeswax candles give off a very subtle scent, burn

for a long time, and are reputed to combat allergies as well.
5. Recommended scented brands:
    a. **Votivo**
    b. **Diptyque**

Head

Plan for the Week Ahead on Sunday. As part of the ini-
tiative to remove personal clutter and use your home
more fully, I want you to take some time to sit down in
your home on Sunday with your date book or calendar
and plan your week ahead. However you like to organize
your to-do lists and appointments, do so before the week
begins and do it in your home.

As you do this, be sure to make yourself comfortable
and observe how you feel. Unlike simply relaxing at home,
this is a personal organizing activity that is also an investment in your own success. Do you have a place where
you can sit and do this comfortably? Do you have everything you need to do this? Pencil? Calendar? How does it
feel to do this at home, within your refuge, instead of first
thing in the morning on your way to work?

Ideally your home is the place where you withdraw
from the world for pleasure, to rest, and in order to work
for yourself. If you don't feel comfortable doing this, take
a look around your home and see what one thing you
can do this week to improve it for next week.

Wake Early and Take a Bath Before Work. Wake early
enough twice this week to take a thirty-minute bath before you go to work. If you want to read in the bath, go
ahead. It is said that no less a personage than Alan
Greenspan, the former chair of the Federal Reserve Board,

takes a long bath *every morning,* during which time he pre-
pares for the day ahead by reading over whatever paperwork he has due that day. It is also said that water stains
on his papers are regularly observed by others during his
daily meetings in the government.

Observe how you feel as you begin to use your house
more fully, taking time to prepare for your daily life outside
of it. Too often our homes become like bus stations, where
we stop between one activity and the next. See if by planning ahead and rising early, you begin to feel even better
about yours.

Optional: Consider a Media Fast for the Next Week. If
you enjoyed the experience of the one-day media fast
last week, consider trying it for the next week as well. If
this is new to you, it will be challenging. It will throw off
all of your normal flow patterns through your home, and
you may find it extremely uncomfortable at times. Stay
with it for the week, and as your flow patterns shift, it will
become easier and easier.

During the week of the media fast, observe how you
think about your evenings. Are they enjoyable or are they
lonely? Observe what you find yourself doing. Do you do
things you haven't done in a long time, or are you at a
loss to fill in the time with enjoyable activities? Observe
what time you find yourself eating dinner and going to
sleep. With the removal of media, you will experience a
fuller relationship with your home. If it isn't satisfying to
you, think about what you could do to improve it throughout the week. If it is highly satisfying to you, think about
how much media you need in your home and if any of
it could be reduced, made smaller, or moved to the
Outbox.

Optional: Straighten Your Desk at Work. As your habits at home change, take a look at your habits at the office as well. This week, take five minutes at the end of each day to straighten up your desk. If you don't have an Outbox in your office, designate one now. During these five minutes put all of your pencils and paper away, put file folders in their proper drawers, and move anything that you can let go of into the Outbox. See what effect this has on the flow of your office, your efficiency, and the relaxation you feel when coming to and leaving work.

At the end of the week, take fifteen minutes and clear your desk. This means that the top of your desk is really clear of all papers. All pens and pencils are in containers and everything is put away. This will require making decisions on items that are waiting for them. Many times we leave things on our desk to remind us that we are working on them or that they are next in line. If this is the case, use a notepad to make detailed notes of those things you wish to remember, and continue to put all files and papers away. On Monday, you can rely on this small notepad to remind you exactly where you were.

One-Room Remedy

Finalize Your Lighting Arrangement. As I've mentioned, most homes are not well lit, which is a shame, because good lighting is a luxury that everyone can afford. This week, I want you to make whatever changes are necessary to ensure that the room you are working on is properly lit. A correctly lit room has at least three unique points of light that vary from bright, concentrated light to soft, ambient light.

Light Flow

When you enter a room, your eye is instinctively drawn to the light sources. Light fixtures also create warmth and visual movement all around them. A room that relies on a single fixture in the ceiling does not allow much movement and draws our gaze up away from where we live.

With good lighting you can create a flow of light throughout your home, which leads the eye through each room and invigorates the space. In a more sophisticated room, even the intensities of the lights vary, from strong light such as reading or task lights to small twinkling lights such as candles and indirect illuminators such as floor or table lamps.

The best lighting is often found in fine restaurants, where lighting designers are fully aware of the flow and visual movement they want to promote. For primary lighting, restaurants use indirect lighting to illuminate a room, with fixtures directed at the walls or ceiling. They will use multiple smaller lights to illuminate specific spots such as tables, wait stations, and bars. Candles on every table are a crowning touch, the small flames creating a twinkling throughout the room. Although restaurants are often darker than you want your home to be, they offer excellent examples of light flow and useful inspiration for the home.

Finally, adding lighting to your home doesn't have to be limited to buying a new table lamp. Lighting can be creative. You can add light in many ways: screwing a light socket to the wall, running an extension cord around the room or under a rug, or having an electrician run new cable through your wall. In the following sections specific rooms and types of lighting are covered. Let this guide you this week and make whatever changes are necessary to improve the lighting in your room.

Living Rooms

Living rooms are usually the largest and therefore require the most light. For a basic configuration, I recommend a table lamp on either side of the couch as well as a reading lamp beside an armchair facing the couch.

More light than this could come from an additional floor lamp or overhead lighting if it is directed against the walls. Far more dramatic and vitalizing for a living room with nice walls is uplighting placed toward the corners and directed up along the wall.

Kitchens

Kitchens should have overhead lighting as well as under-cabinet lighting. While kitchens are the only rooms that really can rely on overhead lighting, under-cabinet lighting warms up the room considerably while allowing for a much better working light when cooking. If you want to install these yourself, under-cabinet lights are easily purchased at hardware stores and lighting shops and can be mounted with two screws.

For the ceiling, track lights that focus on the counters or overhead fixtures that diffuse the light work well. Fluorescent light should be avoided. While many kitchens have fluorescent fixtures installed, they give off a cold, unattractive light and should be replaced whenever possible.

Offices

All workspaces should have a good, bright light to work by. Task lights are most effective and direct glare away from computer screens, but they can often seem too office-like in a home environment. Therefore, I recommend either purchasing a nicely designed task light (one of my favorites is the **Tolomeo Series** from Artemide) or placing one or two small table lamps on either side of the work area. Table lamps lend a very elegant formality to a working desk and take the office feeling out of it.

Dining Rooms

Ideally, dining rooms are lit along the walls by sconces or table lamps while candles light the dinner table itself. When dinner parties are not in progress, I recommend placing an attractive table lamp on the dining table. This will brighten the room, remove the dining room feeling, and allow other activities to take place at this table as well. Chandeliers or pendant lamps are another good way of getting light into the dining room in a way that doesn't take up table space. These can easily be installed by an electrician if your room has an electrical box already in the ceiling.

Hallways

Hallways should have two lights: one overhead ceiling fixture with diffuse light and a strong table lamp to illuminate the Landing Strip. This second light is extremely important, because without it, you will not stop to sort the day's mail in the front hall. This table lamp allows the front hall to work for you.

Bedrooms

Bedrooms should have a reading light on either side of the bed and at least one other light, often on a table opposite the bed. The reading lights should be easy to reach and provide a good light for reading in bed. These lights have a special importance in that they are the last lights you turn out each day.

While table lamps are most beautiful, wall lamps and sconces are very stylish and modern and take up the least space. I have mounted countless wall lamps designed by IKEA in clients' homes to great effect, as well as the more expensive Tolomeo wall sconce by Artemide. For bedrooms where there is not much room around the bed, sconces are an ideal solution.

Closets

All closets should have light in them, but not many do. Closet lighting is easy to install and makes for a very beautiful indirect light when closets are covered with curtains instead of doors. Lighting within also makes it far easier to keep closets organized and free of clutter.

An easy way to install light is to buy a ceramic fixture with a pull chain at your hardware store and, after wiring it with a plug, install it into the ceiling of your closet. The wire can be stapled along the wall, down the side of the door frame, and out to the nearest plug. Wide closets should have two lights, and really big ones three.

For a strong, bright light inside closets, use halogen bulbs. If you prefer to mount your fixtures against the rear wall of your closet (this is useful if there are shelves and you want to light under and above the shelves), using a silver crown bulb will eliminate any glare and give your closet a stylish look.

Dimmers

Dimmers are an essential part of all dining and living rooms. They allow you to take the basic lighting you have and create multiple variations, from bright work lighting to soft party lighting. Dimmers are easy to have installed within your preexisting electrical switches and only cost about $25 apiece at your local hardware store.

There are also dimmers available for table lamps that simply plug into the lamp's cord. These usually sit on the floor and act as an extension cord between your lamp and the plug. These are easy to find in hardware and lighting stores and cost about $15 apiece.

Track Lighting

I like track lighting. Despite its bad reputation in some quarters as a holdover from the swinging '60s or the high-tech '90s, track lighting is extremely practical and can add beautiful, indirect lighting to a room *when aimed at the walls*. People often misuse this type of lighting by directing the individual fixtures into the center of the room. Track lighting should only be used to provide washes of light along your walls, thereby reflecting back into the room the color from your walls.

Track lighting is also relatively cheap and easy to install. Some track lighting can be self-installed with cords carefully stapled to the walls. If there are electrical boxes in your ceiling already, an electrician can install track lighting quickly and easily in a matter of hours. If not, an electrician can also make channels for a new electrical box (but this will be more expensive).

Ropelight, Uplights, and Holiday Lights

Use your imagination when thinking about lighting. Lighting can rarely be overused, and I am constantly finding new lights and new ways to get light into different parts of clients' homes. One recent discovery is called **ropelight**.

Ropelight is made up of many little bulbs connected inside a heavy clear plastic tube about the size of a small hose. It is very flexible, durable, and weatherproof, so you will often see it outside restaurants and clubs, wrapping around the windows or pillars or illuminating a menu on display. Ropelight is useful for illuminating hard-to-reach areas such as the tops of kitchen cabinets, closet floors (for finding shoes), or behind wine racks. Ropelight can be found in lighting and electrical stores. It is sold by the yard and is relatively inexpensive.

Uplights are round canister fixtures that sit on the floor. They direct light up toward the ceiling. These inexpensive fixtures (about $15 each) are useful for illuminating living and dining room walls. They also are beautiful at illuminating curtains beside tall windows. By drawing the eye from the floor to the ceiling, they help to give the appearance of higher ceilings and a bigger room.

Holiday or Christmas lights are cheap and remarkably effective at throwing a festive light into any room. Used like ropelights, they can be taped or stapled inside closets, around kitchen cabinets, or over your front door. If you are having a party, these lights are very striking when attached to the ceiling and allowed to hang straight down. Doing nearly anything with these lights besides wrapping them around a tree works well.

Silver Crown Bulbs

Silver crown bulbs are another great discovery. They are simply regular, clear glass lightbulbs that look as if they have been dipped in silver at the rounded end. The end of the bulb is blocked by a silver coating forcing the light to reflect back toward the wall or the fixture it is in. This means that if you look straight at a crown bulb, you get absolutely no glare in your eyes. They are the perfect indirect lighting source in a simple package!

Crown bulbs are good for bathrooms or any fixture where you might see the bulb. Because they don't really need a shade, many interior designers use them alone on walls in a series. A ceramic fixture with a silver crown bulb reflecting light back along the wall is a very industrial and handsome look.

Halogen Bulbs

Halogen bulbs give off a much brighter light and should be used anyplace where you want to direct the light across a space. For example, halogen bulbs are excellent for under-cabinet kitchen lighting as well as in a hallway where you want the light to shine down on the floor. They are also excellent for uplights, where you want them to shine up toward the ceiling.

Daylight or Full-Spectrum Bulbs

I use regular household soft white bulbs in many instances, but for interiors where there is not much sunlight, I use daylight or full-spectrum bulbs. Manufactured by GE under the name **Reveal** or by the Swedish company **Chromalux,** full-spectrum bulbs cast a bright light that has the same spectrum of light as the sun. I find this light more invigorating, and it has been proven to cheer people up during those dark months of winter when we don't get enough sunlight. These bulbs are also much more expensive, so use them sparingly.

Get Painting. Though you can paint at any time during the Eight-Week Cure, if you plan to do so and haven't started yet, this is the week. You should be ready with a color chosen and paint ordered from the store. All you will need is an uninterrupted stretch of time when the stores are still open (Saturdays are excellent), just in case you run out of anything in the middle of the day.

If you have hired a painter, I recommend that you prepare the room to protect anything valuable. Simply rolling up carpets and moving furniture away from the walls will do most of it. If you have pictures on your walls or any items on windowsills, move these to another room. If you have books on shelves to be painted, moving these to a couch is a good way of keeping them safe. Make sure that your painter covers everything with a tarp and uses a drop cloth over your floors.

Doing It Yourself

If you are doing it yourself, I recommend that you first review how to properly paint a room. Ask for guidance from friends or your local paint store if necessary. I have found one of the best small guides is the pamphlet put out for Martha Stewart's Everyday Paint line at Kmart. Here are a few tips:

1. Use the right nap cover on your roller—thicker for rough surfaces such as brick, thinner for smooth surfaces such as drywall.

2. Use latex paint for all-purpose, low-odor, fast-drying coverage.

3. Use oil paint only for floors, outdoors, or for extra-hard coatings on surfaces such as windowsills and bookcases.

4. Buy and use a small steel brush for cleaning your brushes.

5. Clean your brushes after using them and allow to dry bristles down.

6. With latex paint, brushes can be stored for a few hours without cleaning by wrapping tightly in plastic wrap.

7. If you're using oil paint, brushes can be wrapped in plastic wrap and stored in the freezer overnight.

Painting is significantly more enjoyable if you prepare well and do things in the right order. Here is the basic order that I use every time.

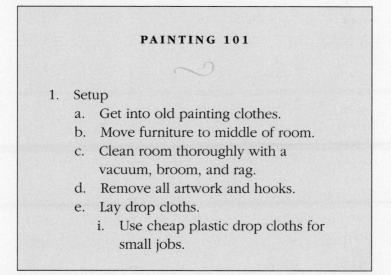

PAINTING 101

1. Setup
   a. Get into old painting clothes.
   b. Move furniture to middle of room.
   c. Clean room thoroughly with a vacuum, broom, and rag.
   d. Remove all artwork and hooks.
   e. Lay drop cloths.
      i. Use cheap plastic drop cloths for small jobs.

        ii.   Tape flooring paper to floor at base of wall for big jobs.

2.   Preparation

    a.   Wash windowsills and very dirty areas.

    b.   Fill all holes with spackle, and sand smooth.

    c.   Sand and scrape rough patches.

3.   Painting from the top down

    a.   Ceiling first

        i.   Use primer first if necessary.

        ii.   Do edges of ceiling with brush.

        iii.   Roll center (one or two coats).

    b.   Walls second

        i.   Use primer first if necessary.

        ii.   Use a brush for all corners and edges by doors, trim, and ceiling.

        iii.   Roll center of walls (two or three coats).

        iv.   For deeper colors and reds, more coats will be needed.

    c.   Trim last

        i.   Start with most complicated area first (i.e., shelves, window frames).

        ii.   Finish with simple runs (baseboards, doorways).

4.   Cleanup

    a.   Put all painting tools away.

    b.   Remove drop cloths.

    c.   Vacuum and clean room of all dust.

    d.   Put furniture back.

    e.   Get out of old painting clothes and take a shower.

Chapter Ten

Week Seven:
Sacred Space

Elizabeth and Colin were not happy with their apartment. In addition, they were not sleeping well, so they had invited me over to give them a full prescription. While their apartment needed some work, their bedroom needed it the most. What I didn't know then but would come to learn later was that they had been trying unsuccessfully to get pregnant for five months.

"We don't know why we're not sleeping very well, but we think it has to do with the fact that the bed squeaks," said Colin.

Elizabeth jumped in. "It's an old bed, and all the pieces are wood. Even when we are just rolling over at night it makes noise."

In taking a look at their bedroom, I noticed a number of things that raised red flags for me: the room was cluttered with magazines from reading in bed, there was laundry that wasn't put away, one of the bedside lamps was in need of repair, and there was a closet door under the bed that was covered in dust. All of this was hidden by the fact that their style and decorative sense was excellent, so the room was not unpleasant.

"I will look at the bed," I told them, "but I have to tell you that this room is a mess. I am not surprised that you aren't sleeping well."

"It does need to be cleaned up, but that isn't a big deal," said Colin.

"For you, maybe," put in Elizabeth, "but it is for me. The problem is that aside from the time we're in bed, we spend so little time in our bedroom that we never really take care of it."

"Then here's your chance. The very fact that you aren't sleeping well should tell you that something is way off in here—besides the bed squeaking. Think of your bedroom as the _most_ important room in your home. Think of it as sacred space."

All of my words were pretty strong, but they looked far stronger reflected in the downcast expressions of both Elizabeth and Colin. I tried to lighten it up.

"I want you to spend some time making this room really nice again. You will need to do cleaning, decluttering, and repairing, all of which shouldn't take more than two to three hours. Can you do that this week?"

"No problem," said Colin.

Elizabeth looked at him. "Don't just say that—you'll be helping with the whole thing," she said with a smile.

I fixed the bed that day, and Elizabeth and Colin took on a Deep Treatment of the room that week. When we spoke again, sleep was no longer a problem, and while Colin attributed it to the fact that the bed was no longer squeaking, Elizabeth attributed it to the room looking and feeling better than it had since they moved in. The bedside lamp had been replaced when it wasn't able to be fixed, the spare closet door under the bed was taken down to a storage locker, and a new basket was purchased to neatly hold a fraction of the magazines that had previously dotted the room.

A few months later I received a call from Colin.

"We're not sleeping well again," he said. "But this time it's not the room's fault."

"What's the matter? Is there something wrong?"

"Well, you know all that stuff you said about the room being a sacred place and how it wasn't being treated like one?"

"Yes."

"Well, I have to admit that I didn't really buy into all that New Age stuff at the time, but now that Elizabeth is pregnant, I think I see what you mean."

"Elizabeth's pregnant? Wow! Congratulations, Colin."

"Thanks, but I want to thank you for helping us. I realize now that I used to treat our bedroom exactly as I had treated my own bedroom in college, as a crash pad where I could retreat and rest. It's much more important than that when you share it with someone."

I agreed with him.

"Now I'd like to have you back over to help with decorating it."

"Why? It's fine now, isn't it?"

"Well, sure, but now that I know the secret, I might as well make it even nicer so we can improve our chances for a second baby."

I could hear Elizabeth in the background laughing, telling him to stop talking nonsense and get off the phone.

Week Seven: Deep Treatment

Bones
Clean the bedroom and related storage.
Buy an air filter for your bedroom.
Buy new sheets, pad, or mattress as needed.

Breath
Declutter the bedroom.
Arrange the bed against the best wall.

Heart
Make sure your bedroom inspires you.

Head
Look into ways to improve your sleep.
Optional: Outfit your bed to reduce allergens.

Week Seven: One-Room Remedy

Clean all workspaces.
Arrange furniture and lighting.
Arrange all electrical cords.
Hang all art.

Deep Treatment

Bones

Clean the Bedroom and Related Storage. While we don't often choose our home based on the bedroom, we should. It is the most important room in your home. It is where you will spend the greatest amount of time when at home and where your health will be most directly affected if you don't sleep well.

As you clean your bedroom this week, don't just clean up extra clothes, old CDs, and shoes, but look for the deep-down dust and allergens that can make you stuffy and restless at night. Wash your sheets, pillows, and all surfaces, being sure to get into all of the places we rarely go, such as under the bed, inside drawers, and in the rear of closets. Here is your checklist:

1. Wash sheets, mattress pad, duvet, blankets, and pillows, etc.
2. Vacuum entire bedroom, including cabinets and especially under bed.
3. Wipe down all surfaces and clean windows.
4. Flip mattress.
5. Buy:
    a. Mattress cover to protect against dust mites and allergens.
    b. Allergen covers for your pillows.
    c. A small, quiet air filter for the bedroom.
    d. Fun or stylish new sheets and pillowcases (if you need a new set).
6. Wash all new purchases, make bed, and straighten room.

Buy an Air Filter for Your Bedroom. With the tremendous amount of time that we spend sleeping, the bedroom is the most important place to have an air purifier. If you don't have one already, buy a small one this week.

If you have ever had an air filter and opened it up after a few months to find out how dirty it has become inside, you know why it is important to use them in our urban environments. City air is dirty. In addition, during the long winter months when we rarely open our windows, there is plenty of dust and stale air generated from within our apartment.

If the noise bothers you, then turn it off while you sleep and run it during the day, or try a fanless purifier such as the **Silent Air** from Hoover.

Buy New Sheets, Pad, or Mattress as Needed. Good bedding is an affordable luxury that every home should have. This week inspect your mattress, pillows, sheets, and comforter. If any of them are hopelessly worn out or have seen better days, move them to the Outbox.

To keep your bed in good shape, turn and flip your mattress once a month and replace your sheets and mattress pad every few years. Mattresses themselves will last a long time if properly taken care of. An average mattress with average daily use should be replaced every eight to ten years.

Breath

Declutter the Bedroom. With small apartments and tight spaces, many people use their bedroom as a storage area, as it is away from the eyes of guests. Others, wanting to have a bigger office space, will put a desk in the bedroom with a computer and telephone where they will work until late at night. All of this comes on top of the fact that many bedrooms already have televisions in them. These are all bad ideas and you should avoid them when you can.

The bedroom should be designed unlike any other room. It should be private, beautiful, peaceful, and clean. It is where you start a family, where you rest from the world, and where you can retreat most peacefully. Therefore, take the time this week to remove everything that is stimulating and will prevent you from getting a good night's rest.

A side note is always needed at this point to answer those who question where sensual fun and eroticism fit into this plan. It is, after all, the bedroom's secondary role, but sexy shouldn't necessarily mean a deep red boudoir with mirrors, candles, and slinky music. If your bedroom is comfortable, private, and beautiful enough to promote good rest, it will perform its other duties with flying colors. A beautiful bedroom *is* sexy, and we will look at this more closely in the following section.

Arrange the Bed Against the Best Wall. When deciding where to place your bed, you want to place your head against a wall and away from the door or windows. If you can, your feet should be oriented toward the door so that you would easily be able to see anyone coming into the room from where you lie. This places you in the most powerful position in the bedroom and keeps you safely away from the strongest energy flows, which can upset your sleep. For ease of use and to balance the room, make sure that there are lights on either side of your bed for reading.

Whenever possible, you want your bedroom to feel open as you enter and to have a feeling of spaciousness and movement. No matter how small your space is, I want you to give yourself a gift and make this room as majestic as possible. Imagine you are a king or queen and this is your bedroom. How would a king or queen place the bed?

Heart

Make Sure Your Bedroom Inspires You. Bedrooms are for more than sleeping. After you have established that your bedroom is clean, comfortable, and healthy, you want it to be pleasant too. In fact, you want it to be more than pleasant—you want it to be sexy.

One client told me she found men's bedrooms incredibly sexy and refused to go out with any guy who still slept in the equivalent of a dorm room. I have heard from a number of male clients as well who appreciate the role beautiful bedrooms play in a romantic encounter. This does not mean that you should clean up your bedroom before going out. This means that you should care enough about your private life to create a beautiful room that will attract others.

Whether single or in a couple, everyone deserves a sexy, beautiful hideaway, and this is your week to make it happen. Here are a few things you can do to help it along:

1. Put your bedside lights on a dimmer.
2. Buy a new set of beautiful sheets and a comforter.
   a. If it is summer, buy light, summery colors.
   b. If it is winter, buy warm, dark colors.
3. Place a bottle of water, a glass, and a small vase of flowers by your bed.
4. Place a small votive or beeswax candle by your bed.

5. Purchase a small, attractive alarm clock for your bedside.
6. Consider installing a headboard at the top of your bed.
7. Purchase a luxurious robe.

Comfort and ease are what you want in the bedroom, so re-create in your own anything you imagine you would love to experience at a spa or fancy hotel.

Choosing Sheets

I recommend splurging on bedding. Buy the nicest, highest-thread-count sheets you can afford, and look for colors that make you happy. When choosing colors, don't buy all the same color; mix it up. Two or three colors at a time work well—you can take inspiration from photographs you see in catalogs or you can try mixing it up yourself. In most cases a little bit of white works well with colors, and every combination you choose should stick to either a warm or a cool palette.

Recommendations:

Stores
    The Company Store
    Overstock.com
    Gaiam.com (organic)
    Linenplace.com
    Purerest.com (organic)
    Designpublic.com

Brands
> **Frette**
> **Matouk**
> **Amenity**
> **Fold**
> **W Hotel**
> **Area**

Head

Look into Ways to Improve Your Sleep. Since the purpose of your bedroom is primarily to get a good night's rest, it is important that you take whatever steps are necessary to ensure this, especially if you have difficulty sleeping.

Light is very disturbing to one's sleep, more so than sound, so your bedroom should be dark at night and no lights should be visible. Curtains and shades work well to cover windows, while some of my clients swear that using a sleeping mask is the best solution.

One can adapt to noise, but it is good to eliminate street and car sounds as well as the loud knocking of pipes in the winter. Insulated city windows are expensive but do an excellent job of cutting down on noise, and there are many who use the gentle white noise of sound machines to mask louder, more unpleasant noises and help them sleep.

While I generally sleep well, I often find it very hard to fall asleep on Sunday night if I have been up late Friday and Saturday. I had many tired and grumpy Mondays, before I discovered the help of **melatonin pills**. Melatonin is a naturally occurring hormone that aids drowsiness, and melatonin supplements boost your natural feeling of drowsiness and allow you to fall asleep if you want to.

Melatonin is considered one of the least toxic substances known and has proven extremely safe when used occasionally in the recommended dosages. I have used them once a week for many years, and they have been very helpful. If you wish to know more about melatonin pills, www.melatonin.com and www.familydoctor.org are good resources.

Optional: Outfit Your Bed to Reduce Allergens. In dusty, dry city apartments, dust mites can become a problem, exacerbating allergies. To really ensure that your bed is as free as possible of these microscopic animals and to relieve any allergies or respiratory problems that you may have, you need to seal your mattress and pillows with covers that are designed to block dust mites. This is also effective if you are allergic to feathers.

Additionally, to protect against man-made toxins that are regularly used in cotton and textile production, replace your sheets and bedding with those made entirely of organic cotton. Eco-friendly bedding, while not always marvelously colorful or stylish, is healthier and noticeably more comfortable to sleep in.

One-Room Remedy

Clean All Workspaces. If 90 percent of painting is prep work, then another big part is cleanup. Whether you are painting or working on some other kind of installation, this is the week to begin cleaning up.

When any interior work ends, a number of things need to happen to finish the job. If they happen all at once, the end of the job can be stressful and the job may end poorly. It is easier if you follow this simple routine for cleaning up. First put away all tools, making sure to clean and organize them so that they are easy to use next time. Then clean up the room, disposing of big pieces such as empty boxes before thoroughly cleaning all floors and surfaces.

Tools First

Taking care of your tools is the first order of business on any job site. When I worked on jobs with contractors, the first thing we did at the end of every day was care for our tools, and then we would clean up the site. Cords were carefully wrapped up, power equipment was broken down, and toolboxes were straightened out and neatly packed up. Not only were we taking care of what were often our own possessions, but even when they were the boss's tools, we were honoring the fact that they had performed a service for us and we needed them not to fail us the next day. Well-kept tools last a long, long time.

Large Cleanup

Careful cleaning of the room you are working in will protect your furniture and the rest of your home. Large items such as boxes, drop cloths, and leftover hardware should be taken care of next. A contractor's garbage bag makes it easier to throw things out without tracking dust and debris through your house, while boxes you plan to recycle should all be taken out of your apartment before you cut them up or break them down.

Small Cleanup

Dust can settle on a room after any work has taken place. A good dusting and vacuuming followed by wiping all surfaces down with a wet rag is advised.

Only after all of this is done should you begin moving furniture back into place.

Arrange Furniture and Lighting. This is the week you want to schedule furniture to arrive. Sooner than this and it will be in your way; later than this and you won't have enough time to comfortably arrange your room.

Rugs

Rugs need to be moved into position first and are often hard to maneuver. Lay your rug pad first and then unfold your rug on top of your pad. If you need to move the rug at all, simply take the edge of the rug on the side, lift it quickly up and down a few times to create an air pillow underneath it, and then pull it toward you. Done correctly, it is extremely easy to move a rug a matter of inches in any direction.

For proper placement, rug edges should either end one inch away from a sofa's legs or end at least halfway under the sofa. It is not necessary for all four legs to be on the rug.

Furniture

Moving furniture is not hard unless it's extremely heavy. If you are trying to move a heavy object alone, however, you can hurt your back, hurt your furniture, or scrape your floors badly. A few tips will help.

1. Before moving dressers, remove the drawers. It is easy to carry the contents of a full dresser drawer by drawer.
2. A rag or a towel under each leg of an armoire or heavy credenza will allow you to slide it safely across a bare floor. Lift gently as you push or pull.

3. If you need to get a bed or sofa through doors and the fit is tight, disassemble these as much as possible. Sofa legs often unscrew, and all bed frames come apart.

4. If you scratch the floor, a small amount of olive oil on a rag will remove slight blemishes.

With your floor plan in front of you, move your furniture into position, largest objects first, and keep checking to see that arrangements are centered in the room. This means that living room furniture is centered on the rug, chairs opposing a sofa are centered on the sofa and coffee table, and no piece is hanging out in space.

In addition, watch that you don't place furniture too tightly. Allow everything some breathing room. Allow the backs of sofas and chairs to "breathe" by not quite touching the wall, while side tables shouldn't be too close to sofas or chairs. Try the arrangement and make sure that it is comfortable. You want everything to allow for plenty of movement while being convenient at the same time.

Lighting

Lighting placement follows your floor plan. Make sure that all cords are hidden sufficiently and that lamp shades are turned with the seam out of your line of sight. Center lamps and place them toward the back on tables so that they leave a pleasing space open for use.

Check your arrangement at night to see what shadows are cast. If you are placing lamps on either side of a couch or chair or are using uplights, stand back and see how they illuminate the wall. Shadows can be very beautiful, but they should be balanced. Harsh or uneven shadows will make the room uncomfortable.

Arrange All Electrical Cords. When everything is in place, wild and tangled electrical cords really can stand out and look awful. Take care of the unpleasant task of straightening, hiding, and sometimes stapling cords to the walls at this time. Once you finish with this room, you are not going to want to climb behind the couch again and solve this problem.

With computers and stereo systems, the best way to control wires is with some type of tie that will bind cords tightly together. Plastic ties that slip around the cords and are self-locking are good, but they must be cut if you want to change anything. There are other types of Velcro wraps and flexible coils that you can easily put on and take off. You can find these at hardware stores or at www. cableorganizer.com.

Hang All Art. Hanging art comes last. This is a pleasure and is the "crowning" of your room, so choose well and don't hang just anything. If you have paintings or photographs that you've just taken down or released from storage, take a hard look at them and make sure they pass muster before you put them back on your wall. Here are a few tips:

1. Don't hang just to fill space.
2. Avoid prints, posters, or other cheap machine-made images.
3. If you don't love it, let it go to the Outbox.
4. Make sure everything matches the color palette of the room in general (warm or cool).
5. Let each wall have one starring piece. The only exceptions are when hanging small pictures on either side of a sofa or bed, or when hanging a series together.

6. Hang big pictures in big spaces (alone) and little pictures in little spaces.

7. Only hang little pictures in big spaces if they are in a group.

When you are figuring out what to hang where, start by laying pictures against the wall. Stand back and see if the shapes and color work with that part of the room. Don't put any hooks in the wall until you have made your decisions as to what and where everything is to be hung.

57 Inches on Center

Most people hang their art too high. In addition, very few manage to arrange their art so that the pieces fit together as a group. The proper way to hang art is to hang everything in your home at 57 inches on center (our average eye level). This is the way art galleries and museums do it, and it works. Hanging all pieces at the same height creates a connection within a group of hung objects and gives every piece the same relationship to the floor.

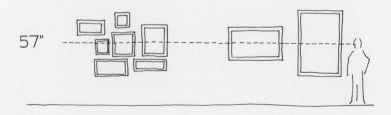

57"

HANGING ART 101.

The phrase "57 inches on center" means that the center of every piece of art is exactly 57 inches from the floor. I recommend using a pencil and a tape measure and following these steps:

1. Make a light mark at 57 inches from the floor.
2. Measure the painting height. If, for example, it's 24 inches tall, you know you want the top of the painting to be 12 inches above your mark, or 69 inches from the floor.
3. Measure the distance from the wire hanger to the top of the frame. If it's 3 inches, for example, you know you want *the hook* to be 9 inches above your mark, or at 66 inches.
4. Make a light mark where the hook should go.
5. Gently hammer the hook and nail in.
6. Hang your painting.

I also recommend that you invest in nice picture hooks, as they will pierce tougher walls more easily, damage your walls less and last far longer. The best traditional hooks I know of are **Ook** picture hooks (www.ooks.com), while **Monkey Hooks** are a neat new invention for rooms with drywall that are strong and can be installed in seconds without using a hammer (www.monkeyhook.com).

Chapter Eleven

Week Eight:
Throwing a Party

"Welcome. Come on in."

Nancy was at the door, dressed beautifully, and her friends were coming in. She had been nervous about having a party in her apartment, and there had been a big rush to finish everything up, but now it looked beautiful. Nancy's work in the formerly green-striped room was complete, and it had paid off, allowing her to serve a buffet in that room, while the rest of the apartment sparkled with candles.

Glowing comments floated around the room as Nancy served champagne.

"Nancy, what a lovely place you have."

"How come you haven't had us over before?"

"What kind of shelving is that? It's totally cool."

Nancy had invited me and then continually introduced me as her "Apartment Therapist." Her friends would then compliment me on my work.

"Oh, it's not my work," I was quick to say. "I was the coach, but Nancy did everything herself."

"Really?" they said, surprised.

Later in the party, Nancy pulled me aside to thank me. "I'm so grateful that you insisted I have this party. You know me—if I hadn't done this, I would have never finished that room," she said, pointing toward the room where the Day-Glo lime green stripes had been.

I was glad she said this, because the party planning had been my only hope for leverage when I saw how long she took deciding on what she liked in her apartment. It really had pushed this project to completion. Just minutes before the guests had arrived, Nancy had put the last few books up on her shelves, and I had been helping screw two reading lights into the wall of her bedroom.

"Now," she said, "as soon as this is over, I want you to come back so that we can work on the next room."

"Great!" I said, sipping my bubbly. "And let's start by planning the next party."

"I'll order the champagne tomorrow," she joked before drifting off to mingle with her guests.

Week Eight: Deep Treatment and One-Room Remedy

General
Find a good recipe and test it.
Prepare your apartment the day before.
Get home early on the day of the party.

Bones
Vacuum the entire apartment and clean all windows.

Breath
Do a final purge for clutter and empty the Outbox.
Arrange the apartment for the best party flow.
Remove your shoes when at home.
Consider improving your audio system and making it smaller.

Heart
Buy fresh flowers.
Turn down the lights and light your candles.
Choose the music ahead of time.
Serve cold drinks immediately.

Head
Cook and eat at home, plan the week ahead, and wake early for a bath.
Optional: Consider removing the television.

This is a big week. You are in the home stretch. In addition to making sure that your project is finished and that all the loose ends are tied up, you are throwing a party, which is a project in itself. By preparing for a party, you will be reviewing everything you have learned during the eight weeks.

Inviting guests over is a very different use of your home. It has more in common with staging a play than it does with living in it each day. Therefore, you want to keep in mind the experience of people who have never been to your home before. What would they notice first? Would they feel comfortable walking in? What would they need to feel more comfortable? Where would they sit? The immediate experience one receives when entering a home sets a tone, so you want to be ready and prepare a number of things in advance.

General

Find a Good Recipe and Test It. The first thing you think about is what food or drink you are going to serve. If you are giving a dinner party, the food is the center of the evening and the most important element of your party. Dinner must be delicious, but it doesn't need to be complicated. Therefore, find a recipe that you like and which doesn't pose too great a difficulty to cook. Test it this week on one of your home cooking nights.

All simple dinner parties should have at least four courses: hors d'oeuvres, salad, main course, and dessert.

Hors d'Oeuvres

This can be simple and store-bought. Cheese and crackers is classic (choose one hard and one soft, or one mild and one pungent). Pâté, olives, and smoked salmon whet the appetite and go well with wine or beer.

Salad

The secret to a good salad begins with good ingredients and a good dressing. Again, keep this simple, as you want to avoid a great deal of prep that will pull you away from your guests.

Oliver's Awesome Dijon Salad Dressing

2 teaspoons sherry vinegar
¼ teaspoon salt
Freshly ground black pepper
1 teaspoon Dijon mustard
1 small clove garlic, peeled and minced
¼ cup extra-virgin olive oil

Combine vinegar, salt, pepper, mustard, and garlic in a bowl and whisk together until blended. Slowly whisk in the olive oil, whisking continually, until the dressing is emulsified.

Main Course

This is where you really go to town. Make this as fancy as you can without requiring too much prep immediately before serving. Simplest of all is pasta. One of my favorite recipes is "Five Lilies," which you can find in Mario Batali's *The Babbo Cookbook*.

Dessert

This should be easy as well as decadent. A simple chocolate mousse can be made days in advance and stored in the freezer, and ice cream or sorbet is always an easy solution.

Orange Pants' Deadly Simple Chocolate Mousse

1 pint heavy cream
½ cup water
3 tablespoons freshly brewed strong coffee
1 tablespoon sugar
6 ounces semi-sweet chocolate chips or pieces
1 egg
1 to 3 tablespoons dark rum or cognac (to taste)

Pour cream into food processor and run until whipped (holding soft peaks). Pour into separate metal bowl and chill in freezer.

In a small saucepan over medium low heat, simmer water, coffee, and sugar until sugar is dissolved.

Place chocolate, egg, and liquor in food processor. With blade running, pour simmered coffee solution into food processor and pulse until chocolate is melted.

Combine chilled whipped cream with chocolate in mixing bowl and pulse gently until all chocolate is folded into the whipped cream.

Pour into small cups or bowls and chill for at least 2 hours before serving.

Drinks

At any party, drinks are important. At a dinner party, I serve a light bubbly such as prosecco ahead of time and offer good wine to go with the meal. Strong drinks will ruin your guests' palate, cutting enjoyment of the meal to come.

For a drinks party, I offer something stronger in addition to wine or prosecco and make it in advance. It is far more pleasant and in keeping with your new role as a host in your home to have drinks made by you than to simply put bottles of beer or wine on ice. Margaritas are extremely festive, social drinks that are suitable for a housewarming and enjoyed by both sexes.

Margaritas to Make Men and Women Giggle

1 cup fresh-squeezed lime juice
1 cup Triple Sec
2 cups silver tequila
4–6 cups ice

Combine lime juice, Triple Sec, and tequila. Add ice. (You can throw in a few of the pressed limes for color.) Let sit 5 minutes. Serve.

Prepare Your Apartment the Day Before. Just as with everything else you have done over the past weeks, preparing ahead of time will allow you to enjoy the week and look forward to the weekend. If you have any purchases to make, make them a day ahead of time. Set your apartment up the day before, almost as if you were having guests over that night.

Get Home Early on the Day of the Party. With all home improvement projects, there is always something that hasn't been done that will need to be taken care of at the end, so try to get home early to finish things up. As you head home you can plan to pick up any last-minute items that you may need, along with party supplies and extra ice.

Bones

Vacuum the Entire Apartment and Clean All Windows. As you revisit the bones of your apartment this week, consider the changes you have made. You have cleaned every room in your apartment thoroughly and removed dust and dirt down to a level that your apartment has probably not known since you moved in. Every surface is clean, every needed repair has been made, and everything works. Everything is ready to be put to use in preparation for guests. Your home is working for you.

How does it feel? Does the air in your home feel more alive and more vital? Is there a different quality to your bookcases, your desk, your chairs?

Has this much cleaning been hard? Is it worth it? How much will you decide to keep up after the Cure? Cleaning is simple work but grows difficult when neglected. A clean apartment is much easier to maintain when you do moderate cleaning each week.

Do you find yourself feeling more energetic this week? Don't be surprised. Even with all the work it takes, your energy is supported by living in a clean environment.

For a final cleaning this week, pass your vacuum

throughout the apartment to give it a dusting, and clean your windows inside and out. If you live in a tall building or the exterior windows are hard to reach yourself, call a window cleaning service and schedule a cleaning this week. This does not cost a great deal (usually around $12 a window), and the difference it will make is significant.

Breath

Do a Final Purge for Clutter and Empty the Outbox. During this time, I hope that you have begun to look at your belongings more closely. I hope that you have experienced the difference between feeling more attached in the beginning and less attached now. It is liberating to experience freedom from your stuff.

This is the last time you will have a chance to put anything else in or take anything out of the Outbox. Before the day of your party, take this final load away to its best destination outside of your home. You can now reclaim the space that has been the Outbox and bring it back into the rest of your home.

Arrange the Apartment for the Best Party Flow. If the flow in your apartment is good, there is very little you will need to do when people come over. As you look around to see where people will put their coats, where they will sit, and where drinks and dinner will be served, consider how much movement your apartment is about to experience and whether it is ready for it. If you have been careful to clear your rooms of extra weight, center them, and pull all of your furniture out slightly so that everything breathes, you will be in good shape. To test a room, walk quickly into, around, and out of it and then try sitting in every seat. If you can do this easily, you have allowed plenty of room for movement.

Parties need movement as much as people do, so if you are giving a dinner party, plan to host it in at least two parts of your apartment. As people come in they should find hors d'oeuvres waiting for them in the living room. You will have your guests move to the dining area when dinner is ready.

Guests love to look around, and since this is a housewarming you will undoubtedly be giving tours. Make sure that every room is neat and well lit. By using your bedroom as a place to store coats, you will be giving them a good opportunity to experience the full extent of any changes you have made in that room.

Remove Your Shoes When at Home. Try taking your shoes off and placing them at the door this week. Removing your shoes at the door is a good habit to get into. It underscores the separation between the outside world and the inside of your home, it is easier on your floors, and it keeps your apartment cleaner. If you feel comfortable asking your guests to remove their shoes, by all means do so. While it can be an inconvenience at the door, it contributes to a more relaxing environment, and your guests will get to share in a new form of respect for your home.

Consider Improving Your Audio System and Making It Smaller. When giving a party, music is important. Make sure ahead of time that your audio system is working well. If you have an old system that needs replacing, consider doing so this week. If you replace it, consider a smaller system with smaller speakers.

I highly recommend small stereos with small cube-shaped speakers for almost any space, including apartments. The sound of these speaker systems, such as the **Bose Acoustimass** system, is so good that there is no longer any reason to waste space with larger boxes. While the receiver is the one component that still requires some size, almost everything else can be purchased smaller with no loss of quality.

This is also a good time to consider a switch to using your computer as your player and organizing your music with a program such as **iTunes**. Reread the section in Week Five for details on how to put this into practice. Being able to arrange good playlists on your computer ahead of time is one of the great advantages of this kind of system.

Heart

Since a party is a highly social event, you will find that the changes you have made to the heart level of your home will be the most noticeable to guests and the most commented on. Take advantage of this. With everything you have learned about balancing color and light, set up your apartment so that it is colorful, warm, and inviting.

Buy Fresh Flowers. All of your experience with flowers gets to shine this week as you choose flowers for every room in your home. By purchasing a few bunches of different flowers, you will have enough to split up and spread around your house. Don't forget the bathroom.

Turn Down the Lights and Light Your Candles. Lower the light before the evening begins and light all of your candles. While lighting can be higher when people arrive, you want to be sure to lower it as the evening progresses. As soon as you announce a move to dinner, this is a good time to work your way around turning off or turning down lamps. If there are any bright lights in other rooms, turn them off. In the kitchen, turn off most of the lights to signal that it is now time to eat.

With all their flickering movement, candles were made for parties, so be sure that you have plenty lit around your apartment. Small tea lights are best for long, safe burning, and I recommend placing them near windows, where they will reflect in the glass, as well as bathrooms, where they will surprise your guests. For more ideas, see Top Party Lighting Ideas in the Appendix.

Choose the Music Ahead of Time. The music you play will have a very powerful emotional influence, and you should choose it carefully. Again, movement and a change of rhythm throughout the evening will contribute to a healthy musical flow. Start fast, then go slow, and end up somewhere in the middle.

The first stage is light and upbeat, as you want to take people's minds off of the day. Latin, big band, and some pop is good for this. The second stage is dinner, so you want to bring the music down to allow for more focused conversation. Instrumental pieces, jazz singers, and classic old-fashioned vocalists work well. The final stage requires a lift in energy as people either prepare to dance, return to the living room, or begin to head home. This is the time for groovier, sexier dance music (for suggested albums, see Top 30 Albums for a Dinner Party in the Appendix).

You don't want to be deciding what to play once your guests have arrived, and you don't want to ask a guest to take over for you either. In preparation, choose two CDs for each stage of the evening.

Serve Cold Drinks Immediately. When the evening finally arrives, your first job is to greet your guests and get them a drink. Knowing exactly what your guests need is the art of hosting, and the first thing they need is something to do. Having an activity puts people at ease, and being given a cold drink immediately serves this purpose well. Don't forget to toast your home!

Head

Cook and Eat at Home, Plan the Week Ahead, and Wake Early for a Bath. In working through the head level of your home, I hope you have seen your home in a new light: as a launching pad for your life in the world. You have been using it more fully, and I hope you have discovered what a calm and comfortable refuge your home can be when it is a steady part of your life.

All of this week's head activities are carried through from the previous two weeks. As you enter your last week consider how these have helped you and how many of them you will continue within the weeks ahead. Which have been new to you? Which have been the most energizing? Which have been the most difficult to stick with? These head activities are different from all the others in that they are all geared toward your non-apartment-related responsibilities. These activities are made possible by all of the work you have done on the lower levels, and they are the most deeply supportive of your successful daily life.

Optional: Consider Removing the Television. If you have reached this final week, enjoyed all of the challenges it has offered you, and would like to go further, consider removing the television entirely from your home. While this may seem like a radical step, adapting to the loss takes place fairly quickly, and you will enjoy unbroken amounts of calm and peaceful time at home.

The television is a tremendously stimulating machine, introducing into the home much more information than we can process. This results in a lethargy that people often mistake for relaxation. For the most part, television viewing does not create relaxation; all it does is suppress the events of the day and whatever has caused your anxiety in the first place. Its most harmful aspect is in the total absorption it creates, stealing you and your attention away from others as well as from the healthy, active life of your apartment. Whenever the television is on, the rest of your apartment is being neglected. By removing it, you will be making a tremendous move toward restoring balance and vitality to your home, and you will feel it in the greater amount of time you have to do things around the house as well as in a more restful sleep.

Congratulations!

Congratulations on reaching the end of your Eight-Week Cure! I very much hope that it has been helpful and illuminating and has helped restore health to your apartment and put the feeling of "home" back into the space you live in. Remember that everything you have learned is now a part of your own experience and can now travel with you. The change you have created in your own space can be shared with friends in their home, or put to use on a camping trip or hotel room. The art of feathering your nest and making a home can be practiced wherever you are.

Because the Eight-Week Cure is meant to be used in a less intense form year round, you will find guidance on the following pages for the weeks ahead. Use this as inspiration and adapt it to your needs. As everyone's daily life can be different, so too can the ways in which you carry on these habits and activities. Above all, remember that your home simply needs to be used regularly. Movement is health. Every day, week, and month, new energy should be coming in your door and old energy going out of it. In this way, your home will always remain beautiful, healthy, and organized for years to come.

Chapter Twelve

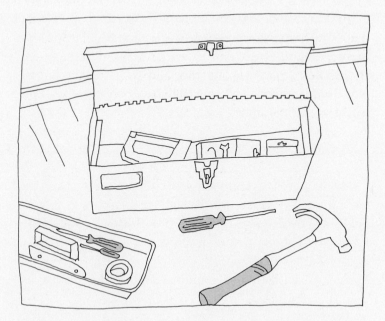

Week Nine and Beyond:
Ongoing Exercise
and Maintenance

Six months after we had finished reworking three rooms at

Nancy's apartment, she e-mailed me out of the blue.

I wanted to let you know that my brother and his wife

came to stay with me this last weekend and they raved

about the new guest room and study.

They were so comfortable that we spent far more time hanging out in the apartment than we usually do when they visit. The changes made such a difference, and I have been continuing them.

I decided to change the lamp shades in the library to red like the carpet, and I added new plants that are still alive! I have been doing my watering every Sunday and cleaning each month, and it is so much easier to keep my apartment in shape this way. Thank you.

Maintaining a healthy, supportive apartment is essentially a daily practice, just like going to the gym or practicing a musical instrument. A little bit each day goes a long way. This continuing work not only strengthens your home, but also increases your own ability to keep it that way. With this in mind, ongoing exercise for your apartment is recommended, loosely following seasonal cycles and other household rhythms.

The following list is for your reference and contains recommendations for scheduling your own maintenance program. You should feel free to adapt it as necessary to best fit your own routine.

General Schedule for Home Maintenance

Daily

1. Make bed.
2. Wash dishes.
3. Put clothes away.
4. Sort mail.
5. Clear answering machine.
6. Clean all kitchen surfaces.
7. Take out full garbage.

Weekly

1. Clear all surfaces (put odds and ends away).
2. Wash clothing, take in dry cleaning.
3. Take out recycling.
4. Change sheets.
5. Water plants.
6. Clean bathroom and kitchen.
7. Quick-vacuum all floors (especially if you have pets).

Monthly

1. Vacuum, sweep, or mop all floors.
2. Flip mattresses.
3. Clear out refrigerator.

Every Three Months

1. Wash windows.
2. Declutter refrigerator, front door, bulletin board, etc.

Every Six Months

1. Spring cleaning (April)
2. Fall cleaning (October)

(Perform Deep Treatment on bones and breath levels: clean and declutter through apartment; change seasonal clothing; clean out drawers, closets, and under-sink storage; purge clothing, extra CDs, books, furniture.)

Yearly

Make one capital improvement to one room (painting, new furniture, rearrangement).

Every Five Years

Repaint main rooms.

Every Ten Years

Make major capital improvement (i.e., kitchen or bathroom makeover, furniture replacement, wall or floor repair).

Appendix

35 Suggestions for a Healthy Home

When you wake in the morning, make your bed.

Make sure the seat is down after you use the toilet.

Always leave the shower curtain pulled across, so that it can dry and not mildew.

Use your kitchen in the morning, even if it is only to have a glass of orange juice.

Take out the recycling when you leave home each morning.

Always include a thank-you note with your rent.

Have your paper delivered. It is cheaper and more efficient.

Always go out of your way to say good morning to your neighbors on the street.

Pick up garbage in front of your building even if it's not yours.

Before you leave the office, take five minutes to clean up your desk.

On Fridays, take fifteen minutes and clear your desk, throwing out or filing all Post-Its, cards, or papers that are old.

Buy flowers for your apartment at least once a week on your way home from work.

Take off your street shoes when you come home. Use house shoes inside your home.

Hang your coat up right away when you come home.

Sort your mail right away when you come home.

Keep all coats, bags, and shoes by the front door.

Use the time just after you get home to run any local errands, such as dry cleaning, pharmacy, or laundry.

Check your messages right away and then erase the tape.

Return all your calls before dinner.

Use a cordless headset to make calls while you cook or straighten up your house.

Don't let your refrigerator fill up with old food.

Always eat on a real plate with a real napkin.

Light a candle when you eat, even if you are alone.

Drink water.

When you are done, clean up and take this opportunity to clean your counters and table. If any counters or tables need oiling, do it right away.

Do all dishes before you go to bed.

Floss each night.

Don't make calls after 9 p.m.

Put all clothes away or in the laundry before going to bed each night.

Take a bath before bed if you have trouble sleeping.
Plan on at least 7½ hours of sleep a night.
Buy good bedding. Invest in a good bed.
Get in bed early and read for 30 minutes.
Only have one book at your bedside at a time. Finish
the books you start.
Give four parties a year.

Top Party Lighting Ideas

The Workhorses

Use white tea lights in great quantities along window
sills, tables, and hallways:

Roly-Poly votives (www.yessupplyco.com)
White sake cups (www.pearlriver.com)
Luna candleholders (www.crateandbarrel.com)
Rotera lanterns for outside (www.ikea-usa.com)
Galej votives (www.ikea-usa.com)

Use pillar candles in small groupings down the middle of
the dining and coffee tables (avoid colored or scented
candles):

Pure white or ivory pillar candles (www.save-on-crafts.
com)
Beeswax pillar candles burn even more beautifully
(www.beeswaxcandles.com)

Dramatic Twists

Attach white Christmas lights to ceiling and allow to
hang straight down

Place uplights along walls or in corners with halogen floods

If you have one, light your fireplace!

Put table and floor lamps on dimmers and keep them low

Party Tricks and Pure Fun

Clementine candles: Cut skin of clementine halfway around. Gently remove fruit. Fill the half of the skin that has center nub with olive oil. Let soak 3 minutes. Light "wick." Make round hole in other half of skin. Gently place on top to make lantern.

Cool Neon Techno Strobes (www.coolneon.com)

Other Resources

Genwax.com

HamptonsStore.com

Save-on-crafts.com

LampsPlus.com

Top 30 Albums for a Dinner Party

Before: Take Their Minds off the Day . . .

Chris Joss: *You've Been Spiked*

Norah Jones: *Feels Like Home*

Pérez Prado: *Havana 3 a.m.*

Maxwell: *Maxwell's Urban Hang Suite*

Esquivel: *Latin-esque* or *Cabaret Mañana*

Herb Alpert and the Tijuana Brass: *Definitive Hits*

Louis Jordan: *Anthology*

Dean Martin: *Greatest Hits*

Everything but the Girl: *Walking Wounded*

Steve Miller Band: *The Joker*

During: Settle Their Stomachs . . .
Chris Connor: *Chris Connor Sings George Gershwin*
Miles Davis: *Kinda Blue*
Dave Brubeck: *Take Five*
Bebel Gilberto: *Tanto Tempo*
John Coltrane: *Ballads*
Sufjan Stevens: *Seven Swans*
Chet Baker: *Chet Baker Sings*
Spain: *The Blue Moods of Spain*
Keith Jarrett: *The Melody at Night, with You*

After: Move Their Feet . . .
Groove Armada: *The Best of Groove Armada*
Maceo Parker: *Life on Planet Groove*
Prince: *The Hits/The B-Sides*
Beck: *Midnite Vultures*
Snoop Doggy Dogg: *Doggystyle*
The Flaming Lips: *Yoshimi Battles the Pink Robots*
Us3: *Hand on the Torch*
The Shins: *Oh, Inverted World*
Zero 7: *Simple Things*
George Michael: *Ladies & Gentlemen: The Best of George Michael*

Send Them to Bed . . .
Sade: *Lovers Rock*

Repair Worksheet

Room	Repair	Solution	Finished

Shopping List

Project:
Budget:
Theme:
Style:

Room/Item	#	Description	Estimated Price

subtotal

tax @ 8.625%

delivery

Incidentals @ 5%

Grand Total

Interior Design Worksheet

Room	Idea	Finished

Bibliography

Covey, Stephen R. *The Seven Habits of Highly Effective People*. New York: Free Press, 1989.

Kingston, Karen. *Creating Sacred Space with Feng Shui*. New York: Broadway Books, 1997.

Schwenk, Theodor. *Sensitive Chaos: The Creation of Flowing Forms in Water and Air*. London: Rudolf Steiner Press, 1990.

Weil, Dr. Andrew. *Eight Weeks to Optimum Health*. New York: Fawcett Columbine, 1997.

Index

About the Author

"One part interior designer, one part life coach," Maxwell Gillingham-Ryan is the founder of Apartment Therapy, a unique interior design practice in the New York metropolitan area. In April 2004, Maxwell, with his brother Oliver, launched apartmenttherapy.com, now one of the most popular and influential design weblogs in the country.

Maxwell is a regular commentator on the new House & Garden Television show *Small Space, Big Style*. Previously, Maxwell appeared on HGTV's *Mission: Organization*. He has been interviewed in various publications, including the *New York Times,* the *New York Post,* the *New York Observer,* the *Wall Street Journal,* and the *Washington Post.*

A former elementary school teacher, he holds a B.A. from Oberlin College, an M.A. from Columbia University, and an M.Ed. from Antioch. He lives in a 250-square foot apartment in New York's West Village with his wife, Sara Kate, a food writer.